IMAGES OF WAR

HITLER'S DEFEAT ON THE WESTERN FRONT 1944-45

RARE PHOTOGRAPHS FROM WARTIME ARCHIVES

Hans Seidler

Pen & Sword
MILITARY

First published in Great Britain in 2019 by
PEN & SWORD MILITARY
An imprint of
Pen & Sword Books Ltd
47 Church Street
Barnsley
South Yorkshire
S70 2AS

ISBN 978-1-52673-157-9

Typeset by Concept, Huddersfield, West Yorkshire HD4 5JL
Printed and bound in India by Replika Press Pvt. Ltd.

Pen & Sword Books Limited incorporates the imprints of Atlas, Archaeology, Aviation, Discovery, Family History, Fiction, History, Maritime, Military, Military Classics, Politics, Select, Transport, True Crime, Air World, Frontline Publishing, Leo Cooper, Remember When, Seaforth Publishing, The Praetorian Press, Wharncliffe Local History, Wharncliffe Transport, Wharncliffe True Crime and White Owl.

For a complete list of Pen & Sword titles please contact
PEN & SWORD BOOKS LIMITED
47 Church Street, Barnsley, South Yorkshire S70 2AS, England
E-mail: enquiries@pen-and-sword.co.uk
Website: www.pen-and-sword.co.uk

Contents

Introduction

Hans Seidler's *Hitler's Defeat on the Western Front 1944–45* is another volume in the popular *Images of War* series. Drawing on rare and previously un-published photographs accompanied by in-depth captions and text, this book is a compelling account of the last year of the German army's fight for survival against overwhelming odds on the Western Front. Each photograph fully captures the strain, chaos and tragedy of those last terrible months of the war as Heer, Waffen-SS, Luftwaffe, Hitlerjugend, Volkssturm and other units, some of which were barely trained conscripts, defended the shores of Normandy, battled across France into Holland, and fought the final battles in a bombed and blasted Reich. In the last year of the war German infantry divisions tried in vain to form some kind of defensive line along a widening front. While exhausted and demoralised, with skeletal units that had been fighting for survival for weeks, they fought back tenaciously causing significant losses to the Allies in a desperate attempt to fend off destruction. What was left of the German army either fought to the death or were captured during Operations Lumberjack and Plunder.

Prelude to Disaster

The opening months of 1944 for the German soldier was a ominous prospect. Out on the Russian and Italian Fronts they had been fighting desperately to maintain cohesion and hold their meagre positions that often saw thousands perish. By May 1944 on the Eastern Front the Wehrmacht were holding a battle line more than 1,400 miles in overall length, which had been severely weakened by the overwhelming strength of the Soviet forces. To make matters worse, during the first half of 1944, troop units were no longer being refitted with replacements to compensate for the large losses sustained. Supplies of equipment and ammunition were so insufficient in some areas of the front that commanders were compelled to issue their men with rations. As a consequence many soldiers had become increasingly aware that they were in the final stages of the war, and this included battle-hardened combatants. They had also realised that they were now fighting an enemy that was far superior to them. As a consequence in a number of sectors of the front, soldiers were able to realistically assess the war situation and save many lives that would have normally been lost fighting to the last man.

Yet, in spite of the adverse situation in which the German soldier was placed during the first half of 1944, he was still strong and determined to fight with courage and skill. By the end of May 1944 the Germans had expended considerable combat efforts lacking sufficient reconnaissance and the necessary support of tanks and heavy weapons to ensure any type of success. Both the Russians and the Allies had constantly outgunned them, and the Luftwaffe air support was almost non-existent. The short summer nights had also caused considerable problems for the men as they only had a few hours of darkness in which to conceal their night marches and construction of field fortifications. Ultimately, the German soldier in the summer of 1944 was ill-prepared to defend against any type of large-scale offensive. The infantry defensive positions relied upon sufficient infantry ammunition supply and the necessary support to ensure that they would able to hold their fortified areas. Without this, the German war effort was doomed. Commanders in the field were fully aware of the significant problems and the difficulties imposed by committing badly equipped soldiers to defend the depleted lines of defence. However, in the end, they had no other choice than to order their troops to fight with whatever they had at their disposal.

To make matters worse, the German soldiers had the added worry of an imminent threat of invasion from the west, which would drain resources from an already depleted Eastern and Southern Front. In a drastic attempt to pre-empt an invasion Hitler had ordered the defence of North-West Europe. During the first half of 1944 along the vast sandy beaches of northern France, beach obstacles and heavy fortifications were erected. Yet, in the German High Command there were differing opinions where the probable Allied landing site would be. Some anticipated that the Allies would mount a number of simultaneous attacks, while others believed the most likely landings would either be along the shores of Normandy or Pas de Calais.

To defend these areas under Field Marshal Erwin Rommel's Army Group B, General Dollmann's 7th Army were moved to the Normandy area and General Hans von Salmuth's 15th Army around Calais, along with General Schweppenburg's Panzer Group West. By late May there were an estimated 600,000 beach obstacles laid in both areas with thousands of troops moved to coastal areas, or what was known by the Germans as the 'killing zone'. Yet, despite the build-up of forces, the Germans that arrived in these areas were either worn out and under strength from years of continuous battle or undertrained conscripts hastily drafted in. These men were now expected to defend northern France from the largest amphibious invasion in history.

Chapter One

Defending Northern France

The German infantry divisions that were mobilised in France during the summer of 1944 had gone through a series of changes and modifications. Many of the infantry divisions had been re-designated as Panzergrenadier divisions. Although having an armoured designation, the Panzergrenadier division was still technically an infantry formation. However, unlike a normal infantry division there was a higher than usual attachment of armoured vehicles. A typical Panzergrenadier division had at least one battalion of infantry that were transported to the forward edge of the battlefield by Sd.Kfz.251 halftracks and various armoured support provided by its own StuG battalion. A typical Panzergrenadier division normally comprised an HQ company, a motorised engineer battalion and two Panzergrenadier regiments.

Other modifications included the removal of the reconnaissance battalion and replacement with a bicycle mounted reconnaissance platoon within every regiment. The anti-tank battalion was modified too, making it more or less motorised and comprising of an anti-tank company equipped with Jagdpanzer IVs, Hetzers or StuGs, and supported by a motorised anti-tank company of PaK and FlaK guns. The engineer battalion also took over the responsibility of the heavy weapons company. It comprised of three engineer companies, each equipped with mortars, heavy machine guns and portable flamethrowers. The heavy weapons in the engineer battalion were normally mounted in trucks, but by 1944 they were predominately pulled by animal draught, while the troops would be mounted on bicycles.

At regimental level an anti-tank company was added. This consisted of a platoon equipped with PaK guns and soldiers armed with the deadly Panzerfaust. As for the infantry battalions, they were equipped with standard and heavy mortars.

By the time the Allied attack began along the shores of Normandy on 6 June 1944, the German defenders had received absolutely no warning until the first enemy shots were fired at them. The 15th Army had already been put on maximum alert while the 7th Army was not and so could not begin a counter attack. Three panzer divisions were within striking distance, but not one of them were ordered to the invasion beaches. Instead, the German 352nd Infantry Division at Omaha Beach, the 709th Static Division at Utah, and the 716th Static Division at Gold, June and Sword Beach were left to try and repel the Allies. Many of the troops employed for coastal defences had hardly any battle experience or proper training. Despite being poorly organised and lacking sufficient weapons, they were dedicated to preventing and delaying the advancing Allies obtaining a foothold along the beaches. From their slit trenches, concrete bunkers, pillboxes, mortar pits, Nebelwerfer positions, machine gun nests and artillery bunkers, the Germans tried their best to hold on to the coastal strong points. As a consequence, parts of the coastal region, especially Omaha, saw massive Allied casualties on the first day. However, in spite of the German coastal troops fervent attempts at trying to repel its enemy back into the sea, the Allies were too strong. Much of the German front had been decimated, forcing what was left of its battered and exhausted men to withdraw and take up arms inland. Within weeks the 352nd Division was so badly damaged it was considered no longer capable of operating as a division, and its remnants were simply thrown into various ad hoc battle groups. As for the 709th Static Division, it had been waging a battle of attrition on the Cherbourg Peninsula and had sustained 4,000 casualties from an initial strength of over 12,000 men. Its commander, General von Schlieben surrendered 'Fortress' Cherbourg to the Americans on 29 June 1944. The 716th Static Division, which had fought defensively around Caen and Villers-Bocage, was removed from frontline combat after almost being destroyed by the heavy fighting.

Within two weeks of the invasion, the 7th Army had lost some 97,000 men, including five generals. On 28 June, General Dollmann died of a heart attack. As for the German 15th Army, it had been eventually released from the Calais area and rushed west to support the 7th Army. However, under merciless ground and aerial attacks, both the 7th and 15th Armies were forced to withdraw through Normandy. By the end of July, the 7th Army's weakened left wing was flattened by a massive Allied aerial bombardment and then attacked and smashed to pieces by the US 1st Army. What was left of the German Army was forced to withdraw where it attempted an unsuccessful counter-attack around Falaise.

It was here around Falaise that the decisive battle of Normandy would be fought. German Army Group B, with the 7th Army and the 5th Panzer Army (formerly Panzergruppe West) were encircled by the Allies in the 'Falaise Gap', or 'Pocket'. The battle resulted in the destruction of Army Group B west of the Seine with 450,000 German troops captured or killed. In the panic and confusion that preceded the army's annihilation, its remnants abandoned what heavy equipment they had left and escaped from the Pocket, retreating eastward to the German border.

Although receiving a heavy mauling from constant attacks, the 15th Army managed to escape the slaughter and withdraw the bulk of its men and equipment to the area where it had been stationed initially for invasion, north of the Seine, and into Belgium.

It would now be Belgium and Holland that would bear the brunt of fanatical German resistance, where it would see some of the bloodiest fighting on the Western Front in 1944.

Defensive positions along the Normandy coast in May 1944, prior to the Allied amphibious invasion of Northern France days later. Here a Wehrmacht soldier emerges from his trench wearing standard issue greatcoat, M35 steel helmet and the usual rifleman's equipment and weapons: the army enlisted man's leather belt, M1939 infantry leather support straps, two rifle ammunition pouches, and an M1924 stick grenade and the standard Karabiner 98K bolt action rifle.

A soldier in a defensive position inside a trench. His Karabiner 98K rifle is perched at the ready and an M1924 stick grenade lays next to him in preparation. Note how well concealed the soldier is. Strapped around the body of the soldier's steel helmet is a rubber band which is holding the foliage place. This was the most popular means of securing foliage to the helmet. Troops used a variety of other methods including chicken wire.

At a railway siding three soldiers pose for the camera, standing in front of railcars in France in May 1944. By this period of the war supplying coastal units by rail was a very volatile and risky operation. Constantly German supply lines were either being attacked by air or by French resistance groups.

A Panther Ausf.G rolls through a Belgium town. By 1944 the disparity of armoured vehicles meant that Panzers like the Panther had to wage continuous defensive battles in order to wear down the enemy in a war of attrition.

A FlaK gunner surveying his position from a halftrack. Mounted on the back of the vehicles is a 2cm FlaK 38 quadruple mount. This gun could unleash a hurricane of fire and was able to discharge 1,800 rounds per minute from all four of its barrels. This lethal weapon had two operators, one who fired the top left and bottom right guns while the other fired the top right and bottom left guns. The loader could quickly change the magazines while the others continued to fire.

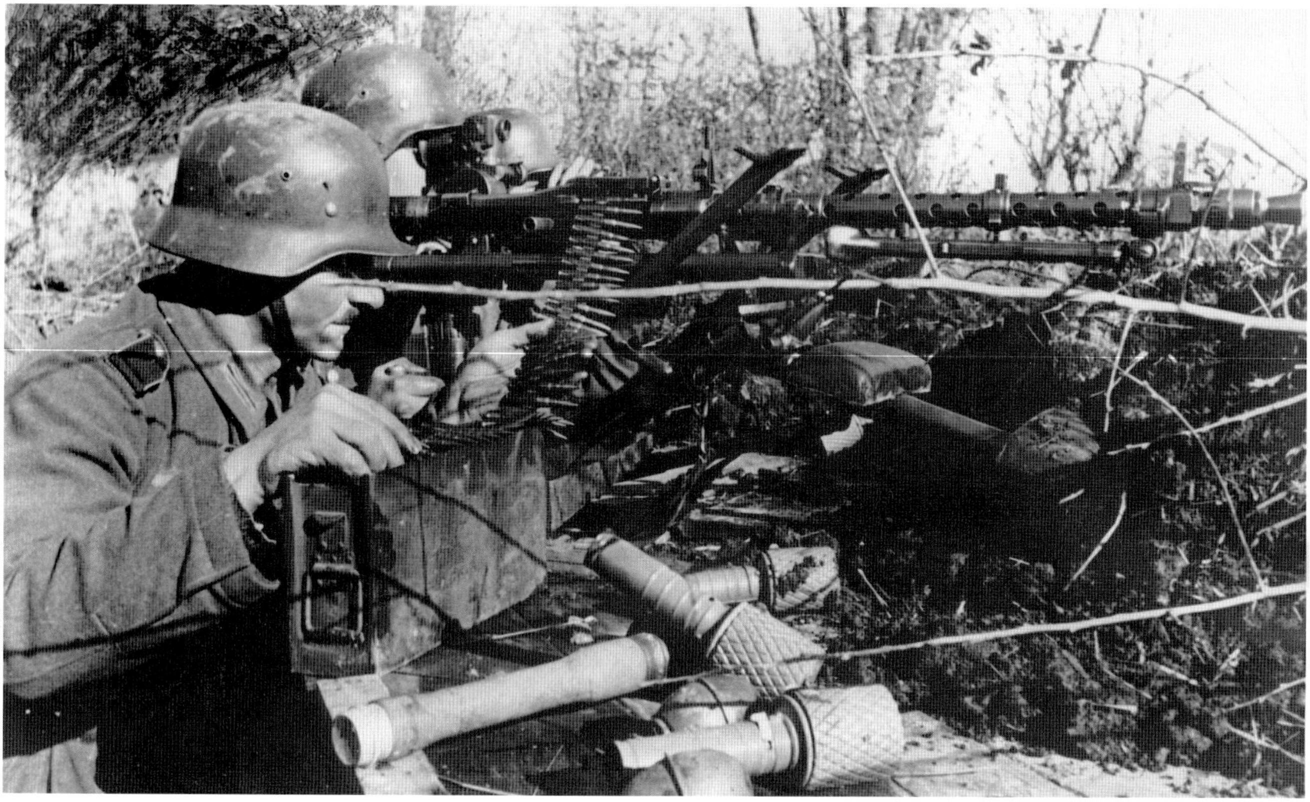

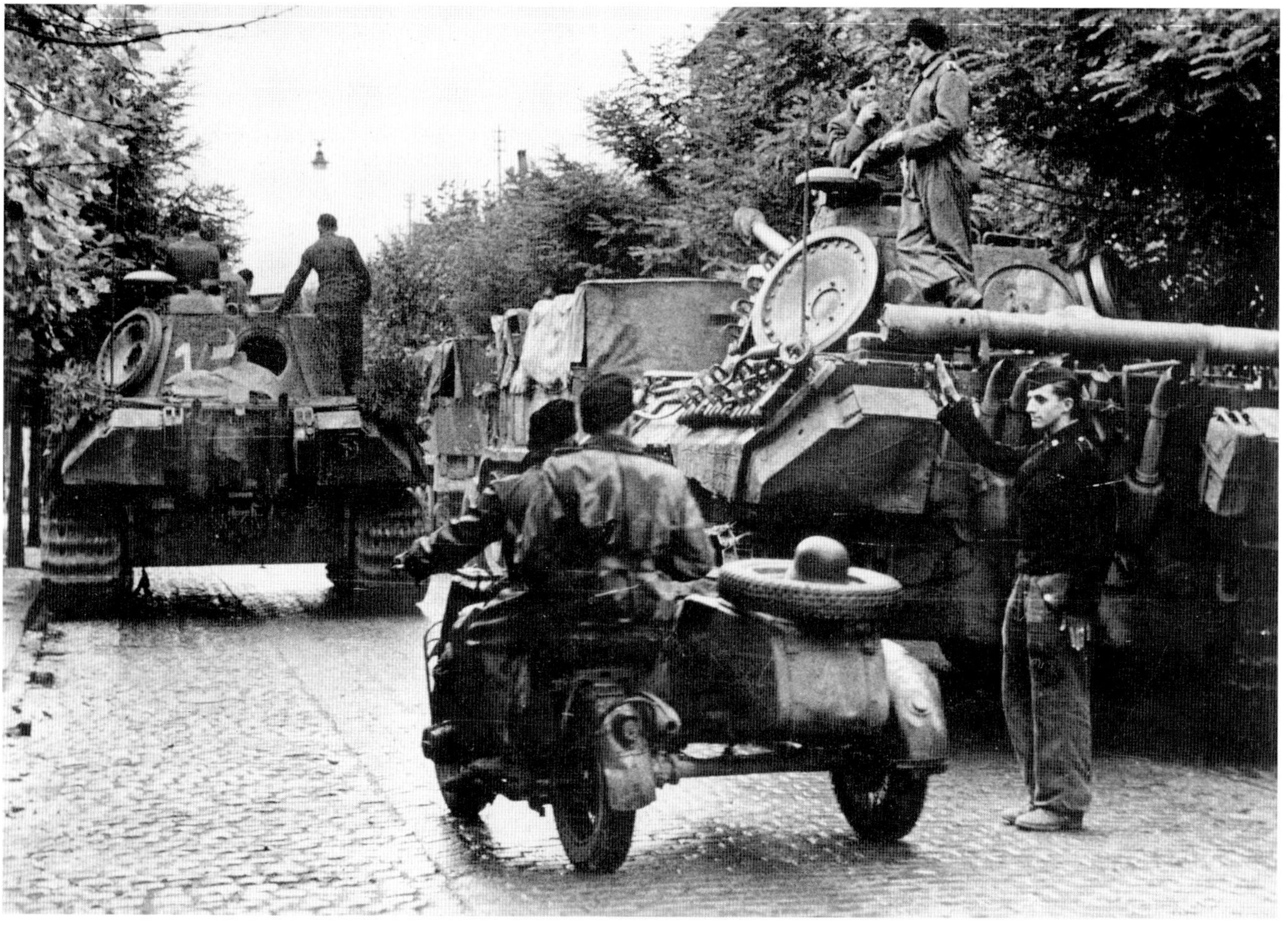

Troops being loaded onto an infantry truck for frontline positions during operations in France. The soldiers have back-packed as much gear as possible in order to endure long periods dug in.

(**Opposite, above**) In a defensive position a well concealed MG34 machine gun crew can be seen with their weapon attached to a Lafette 34 sustained fire mount with optical sight. Note the special pads on the front of the tripod. These were specifically used when the weapon was being carried on the carrier's back. The pads would allow the carrier some reasonable comfort. Each infantry battalion contained an MG kompanie which fielded eight MG34 heavy machine guns on the sustained fire mount. A heavy machine gun squad often consisted of six men.

(**Opposite, below**) An interesting photograph showing a Panther Ausf.G and a Panther Ausf.A from I Panzer-Regiment 24 of 116th Panzer Division. The division fought hard in the Normandy campaign without its Panzer Abteilung, which had been transferred to Panzer-Brigade 111 in the spring of 1944.

A large, bright flash indicates the photographer has caught this 8.8cm FlaK at the moment of firing. Note the Sd.Ah.201 limber unit parked near the gun position in order to quickly limber the weapon back up and move it to another area.

Three photographs showing a soldier armed with the lethal Panzerschreck or tank destroyer. The popular name given by the troops for this weapon was the Raketen Panzerbuchse or rocket tank rifle, abbreviated to RPzB. It was an 8.8cm reusable anti-tank rocket launcher developed during the latter half of the war. Another popular nickname was Ofenrohr or stove pipe.

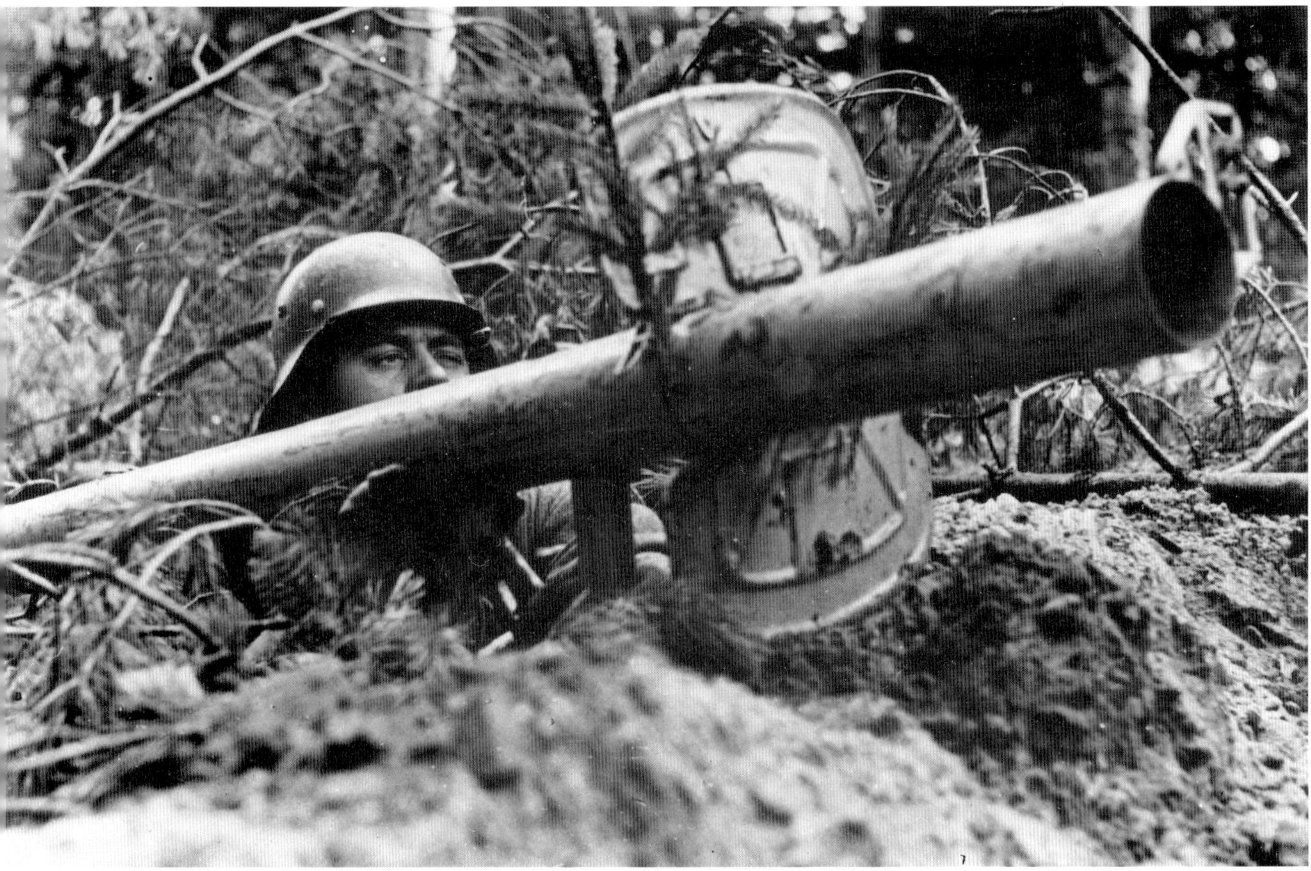

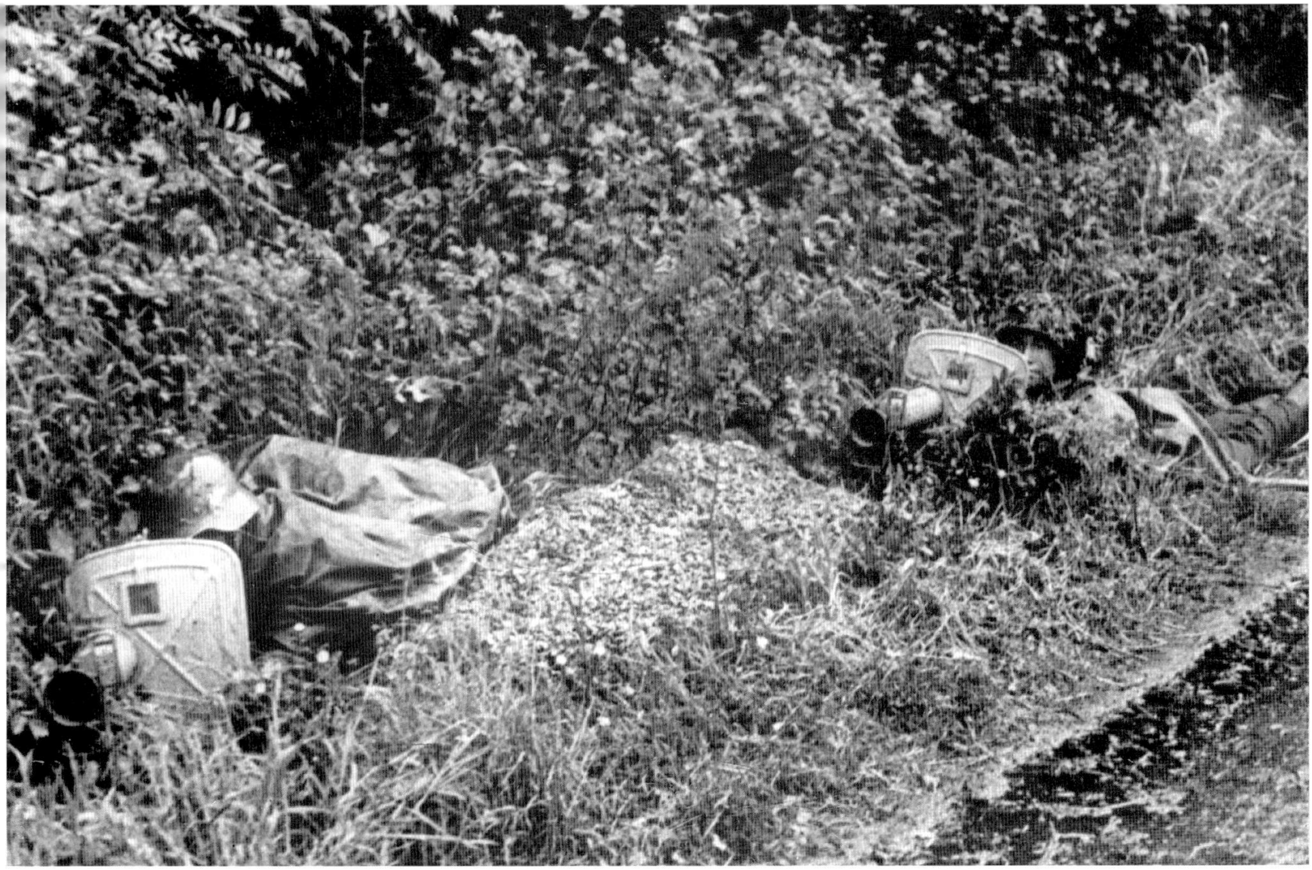

(**Above**) This 8.8cm FlaK has been caught on camera in full recoil just before the semi-automatic breech block has opened to eject the spent shell case. The ammunition handlers each have new projectiles at the ready with a further supply stacked nearby in the usual three-round wicker ammunition boxes. Note the Sd.Ah.202 limber unit partly seen in the photograph.

(**Opposite, above**) A long column of infantry supply trucks negotiating a road somewhere along the French coast in the summer of 1944.

(**Opposite, below**) Tiger tank crew of the Schwere Panzer-Abteilung 503 converse next to their Tiger during operations in Normandy in July 1944. This heavy Panzer battalion was an independent battalion sized unit assigned to a single corps, but deployed according to battlefield conditions. The Schwere Panzer-Abteilung 503 saw extensive fighting in Normandy and was almost decimated by August during Operation Goodwood.

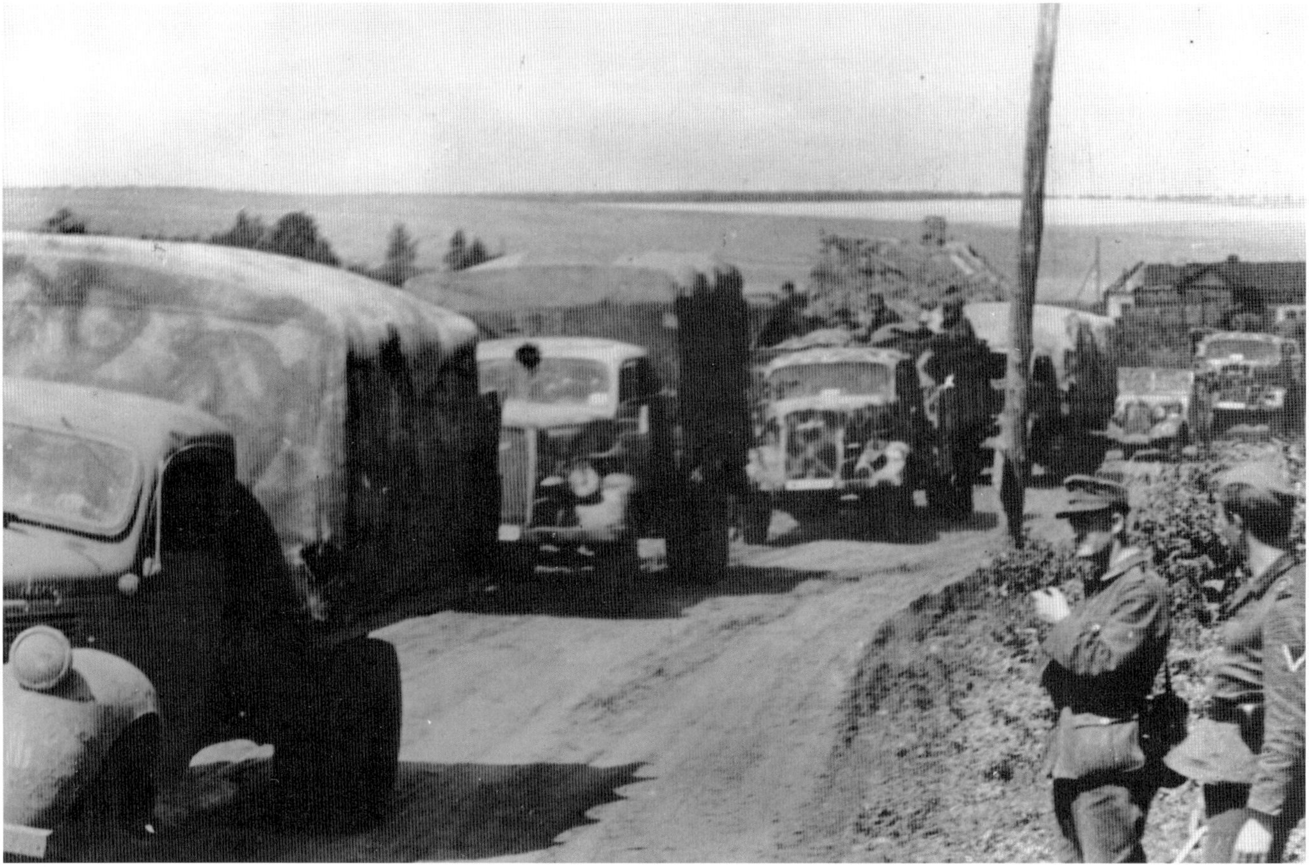

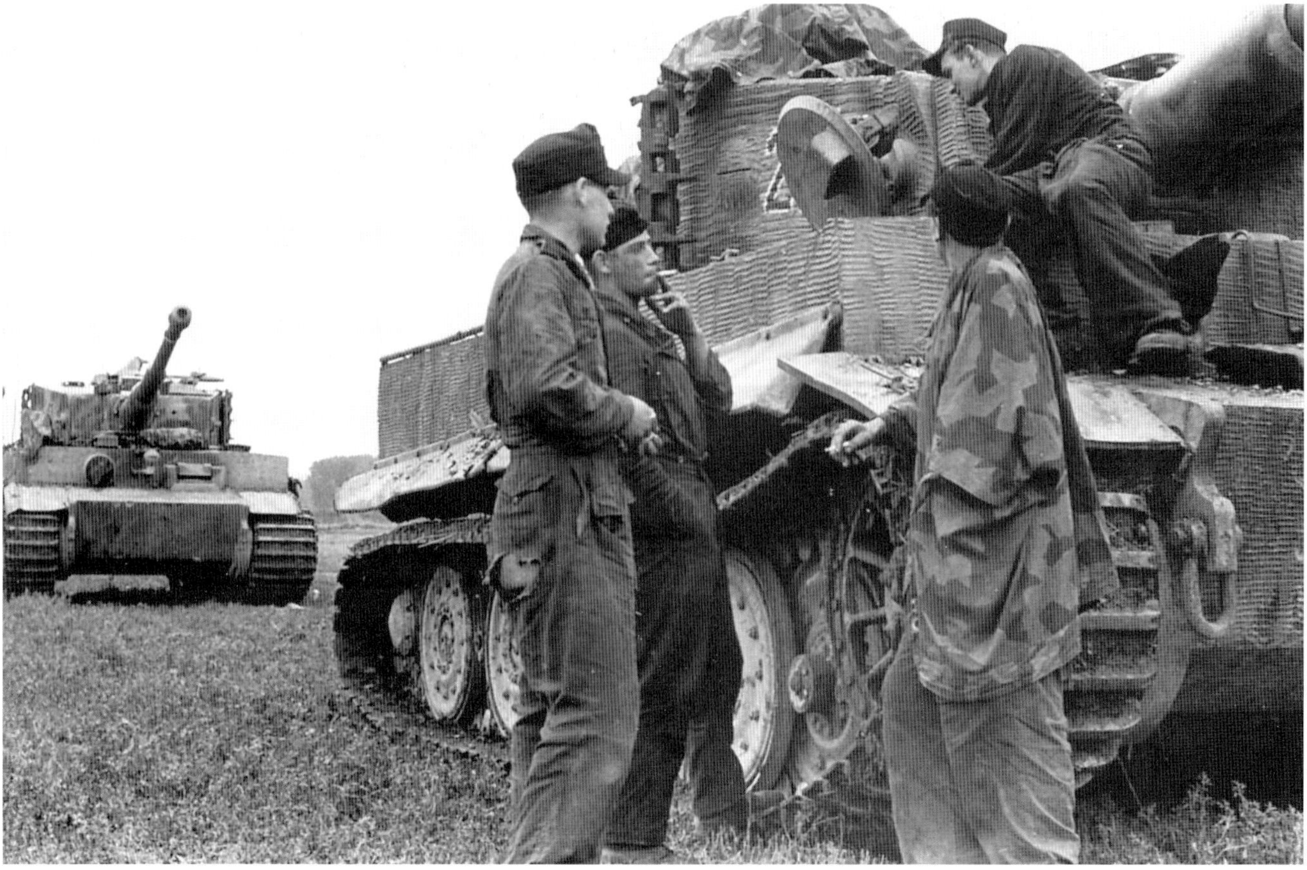

(**Above**) While the Waffen-SS gunner takes aim with this well concealed 7.5cm PaK40, the loader can be seen working the breech-block. The gun appears to be well sited among the trees and some wood has given the crew a good working platform.

(**Opposite, above**) Next to a halted StuG.III Ausf.G, an assault gun crew converse with other armoured personnel on a road in Normandy in the summer of 1944. By mid-1944 the StuG.III had become a very popular assault gun on the battlefield and was mass-produced in order to try and contain the enemy. The vehicles had initially provided crucial mobile fire support to the infantry and also proved their worth as an anti-tank weapon. However, as the Western Front further receded the StuG was primarily used as an anti-tank weapon, thus depriving the infantry of vital fire support.

(**Opposite, below**) A familiar site showing Waffen-SS soldiers sweeping across a field in full battlefield dress. They have purposely spread themselves out in a V-formation in order to reduce battlefield casualties if attacked.

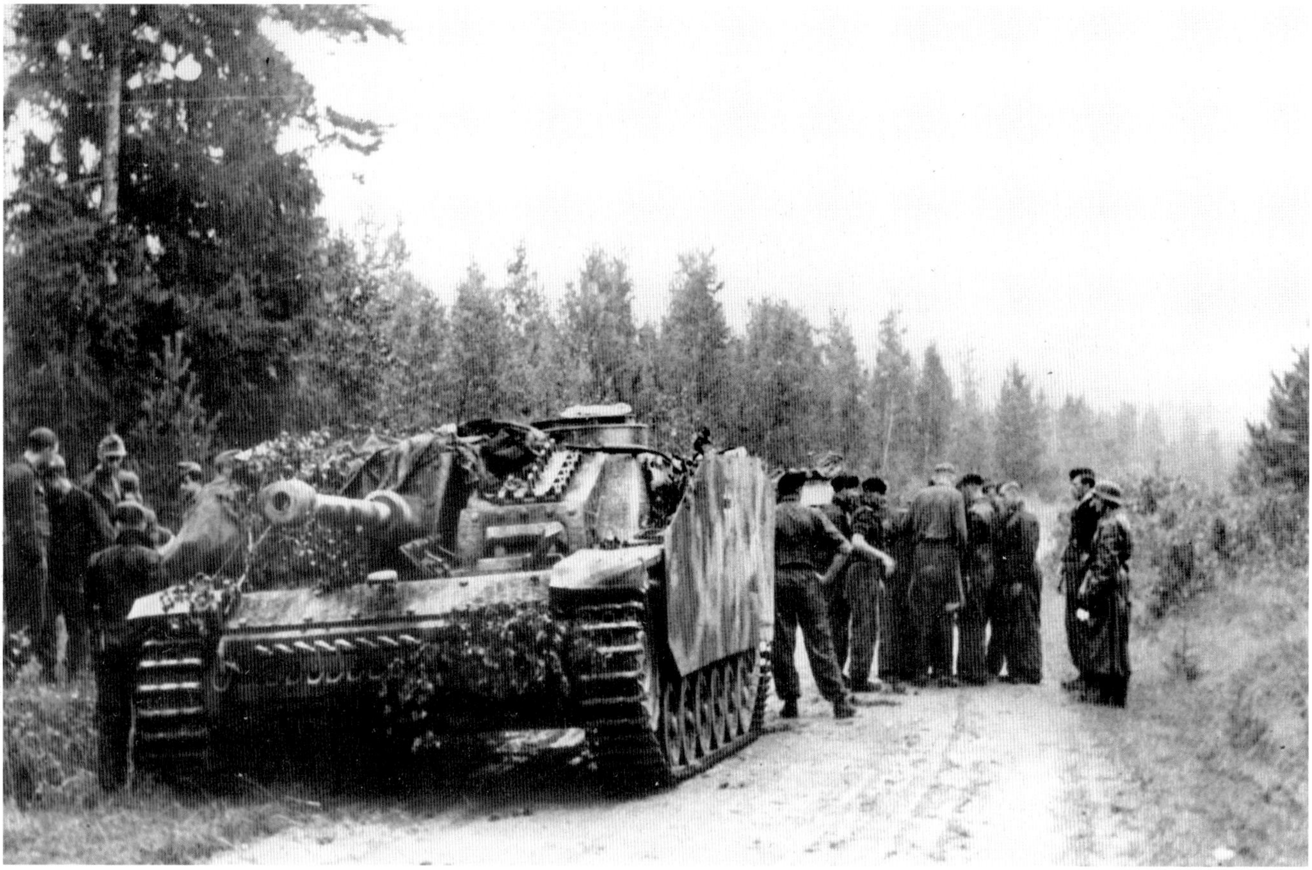

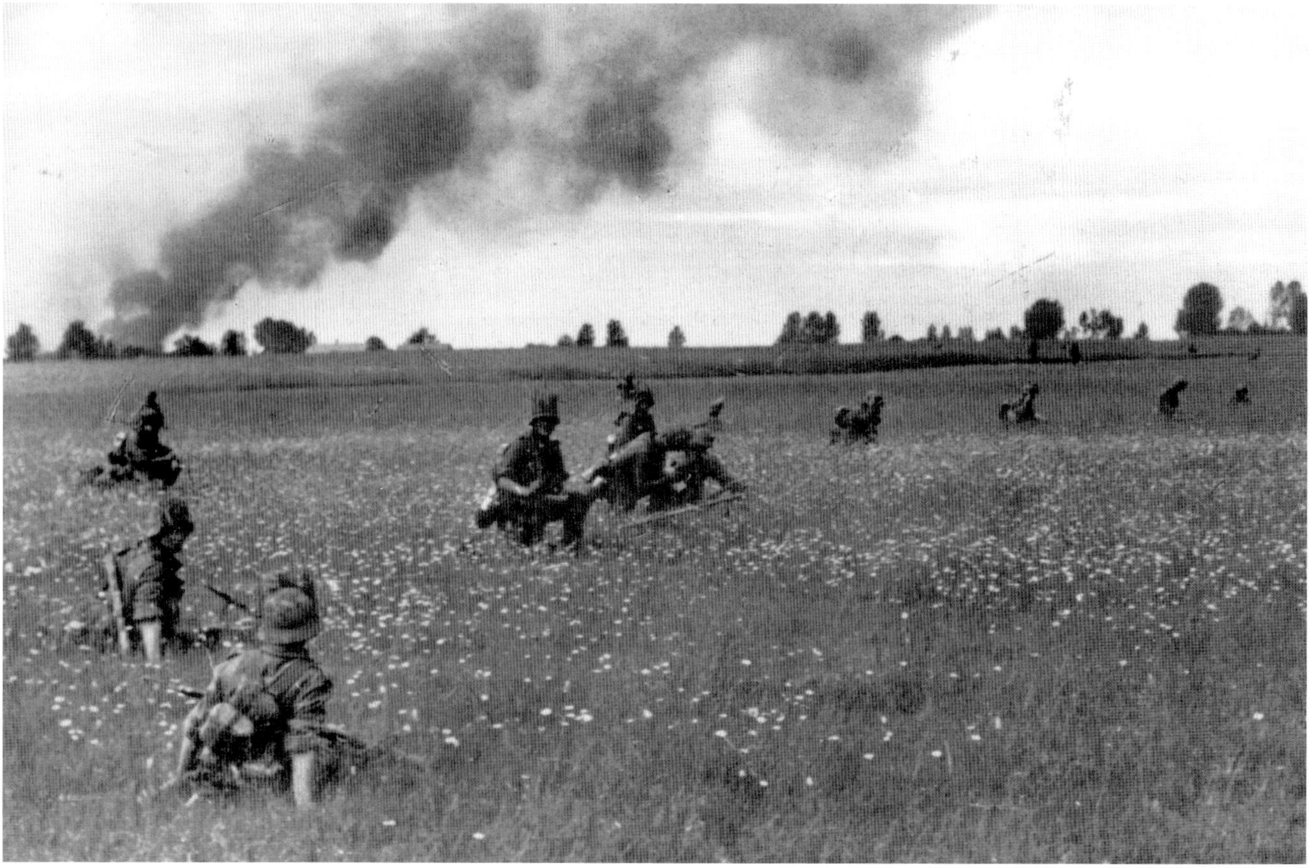

A Wehrmacht soldier armed with a P08 Luger pistol and M24 stick grenade moves forward. Behind him an NCO can be seen armed with the MP40 machine pistol.

A well concealed halftrack mounting what appears to be a FlaK gun. A good coverage of saplings have been applied in order to break up the distinctive shape of the vehicle to help disguise it from aerial and ground recognition. By this period of the war, virtually all German vehicles were camouflaged in order to reduce being attacked during day light hours.

(**Above**) A 3.7cm FlaK gun mounted on top of a halftrack during operations in France. Often the side gun platforms were folded down to provide additional space for the crew to manoeuvre around the gun. Note the ammunition boxes attached to the sides.

(**Opposite, above**) Fallschirmjäger preparing their PaK 40 for a fire mission against the enemy. The PaK 40, although effective against almost every Allied tank, was much heavier than the PaK 38. This meant it decreased mobility on the battlefield, making it almost impossible to move from one position to another without an artillery tractor.

(**Opposite, below**) A 10.5cm field howitzer crew out in the field. The 10.5cm provided units with a relatively effective mobile base of fire. It was primarily the artillery regiments that were given the task of destroying enemy positions and fortified defences and conducting counter-battery fire prior to an armoured assault.

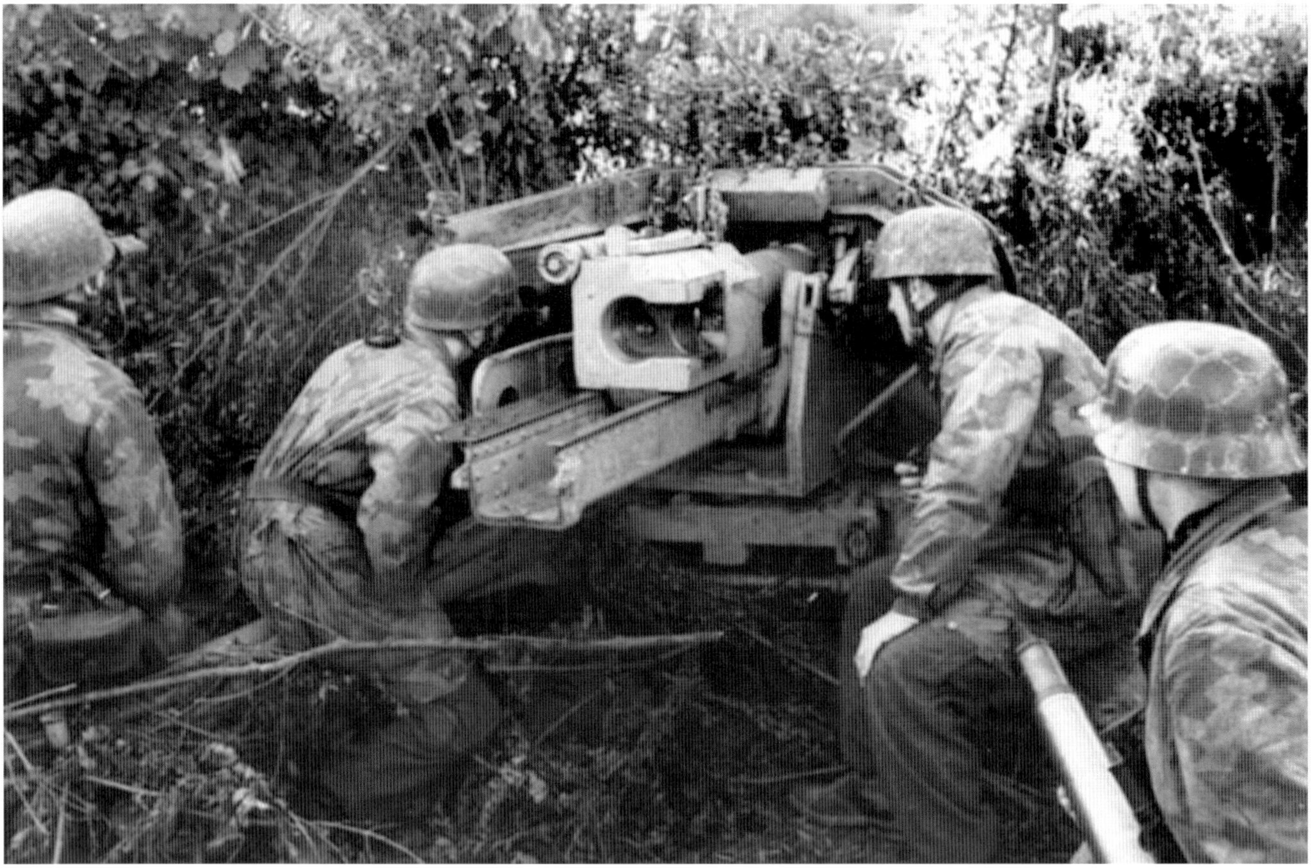

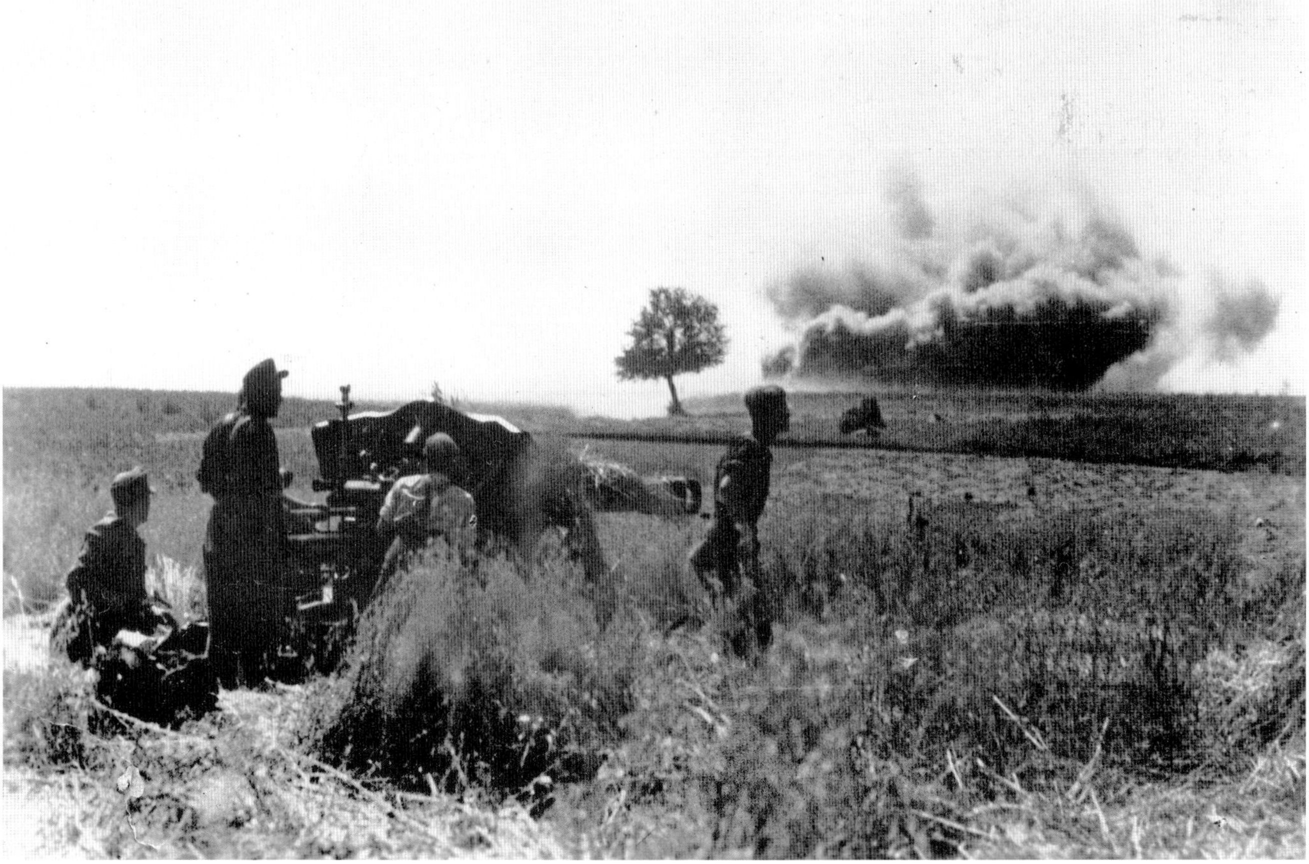

A young Hitlerjugend soldier in full summer camouflage lays out a national flag for aerial recognition. He can be seen placing rocks on the flag in order to prevent it from blowing in the wind.

During a pause in fighting, a shirtless gunner can be seen tucking into his rations while standing next to his 8.8cm FlaK gun. Note the aimer wearing headphones in order to collect information on the location of the enemy.

(**Above**) Luftwaffe field division truppen preparing a Panzerfaust for action. By 1944 the size of the Luftwaffe's land based combat elements far surpassed that of the aerial. It boasted to have a huge FlaK branch and a massive ground presence of Luftwaffe troops fighting alongside the army. It eventually included twenty-one field divisions plus countless smaller regiments, many of which fought in a number of large battles. However, like every part of the German fighting force, it was unable to change the course of the war. Consequently, it soon succumbed to a high loss rate on the battlefield, until its units were fighting piecemeal along with other broken elements of the German Army.

(**Opposite, above**) This 8.8cm FlaK 18 can be seen during a fire mission in a field. The gun is identified as a FlaK18 by the limbers for the Sd.Ah.201 which only fitted this gun. This piece has only just been fired as smoke is evident coming out of the breech.

(**Opposite, below**) By 1944 the German infantry division had gone through a series of changes and had been modified and reorganised. The reconnaissance battalion for instance was removed and replaced by a bicycle-mounted reconnaissance platoon within every regiment. Here in this photograph a reconnaissance platoon can be seen operating along a French road.

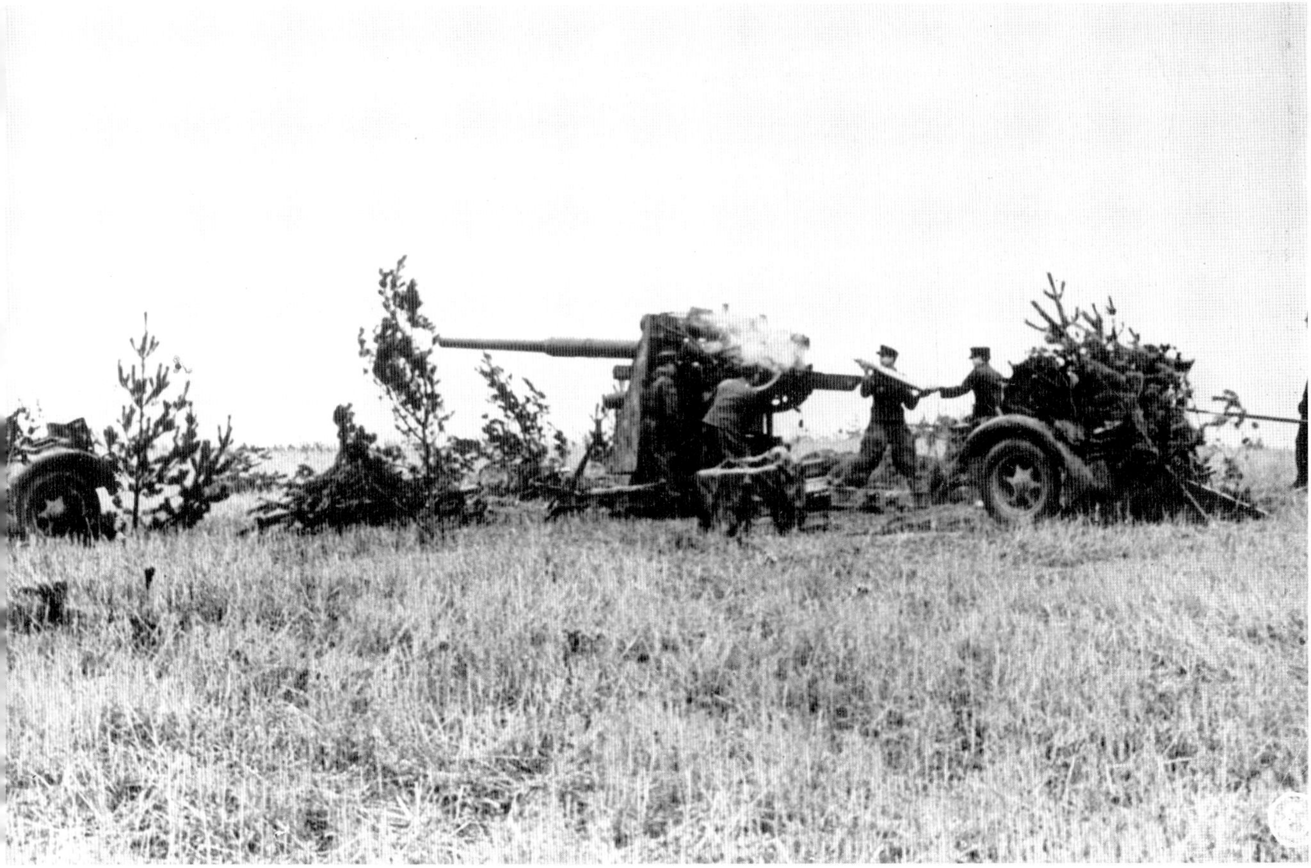

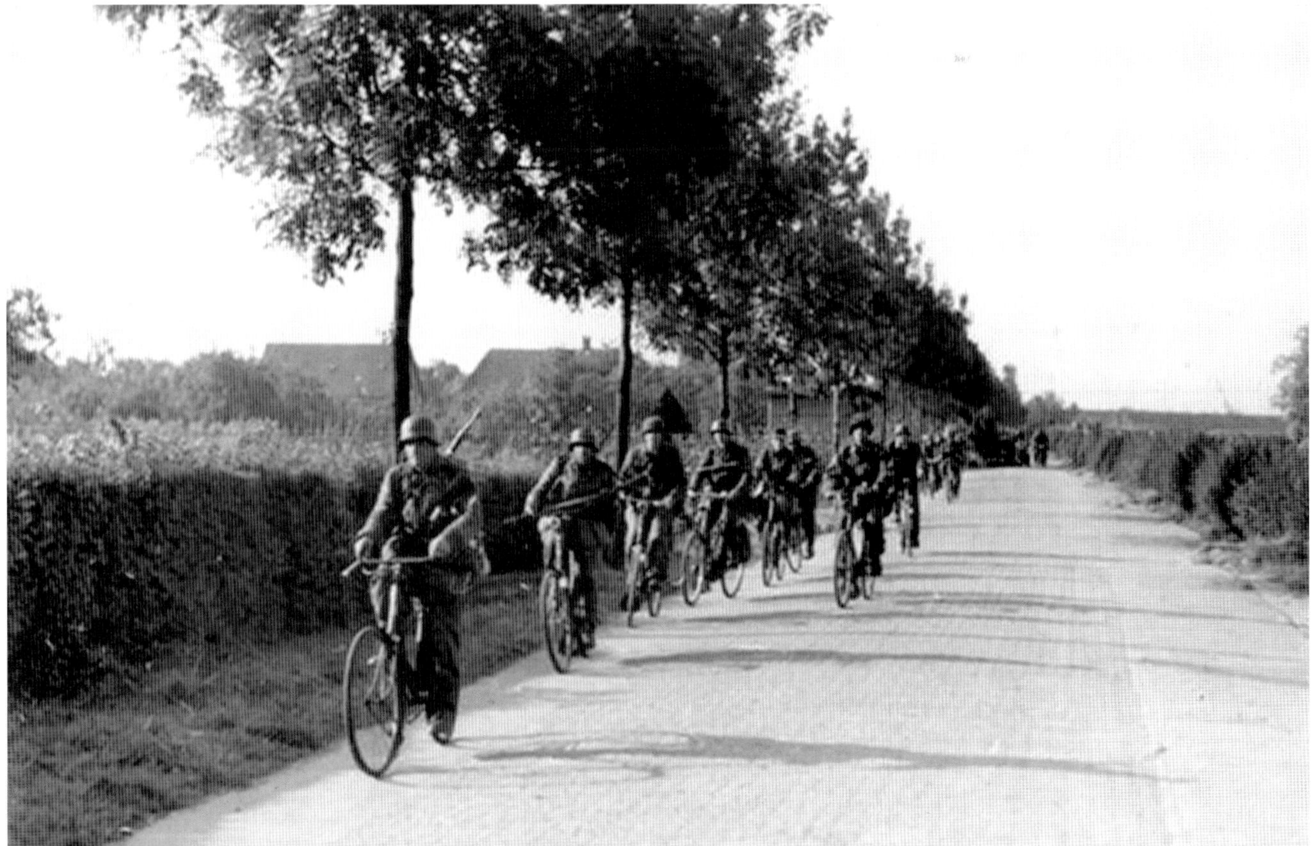

Two photographs taken in sequence of a knocked out British Infantry Mk IV (A22) Churchill tank, which was a heavy infantry tank. Churchills saw widespread action in Normandy and were very versatile machines. The first image shows Waffen-SS soldiers surveying the vehicle.

A photograph captures the moment a FlaK gunner is about to load his projectile into the breech of the 8.8cm FlaK gun. The gunner is wearing the splinter pattern suit jacket, and a pair of mittens to protect his hands from the hot discarded shell cases that are ejected from the breech.

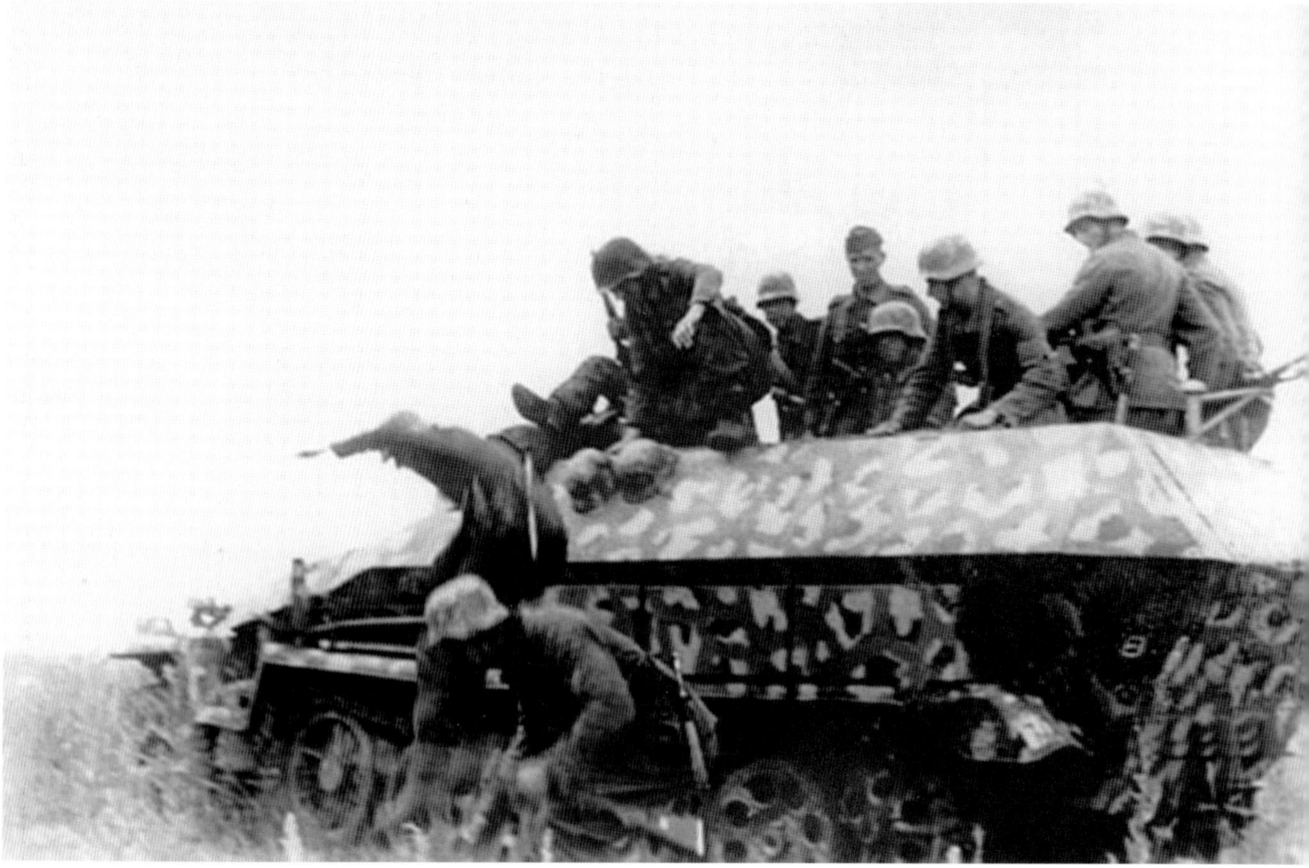

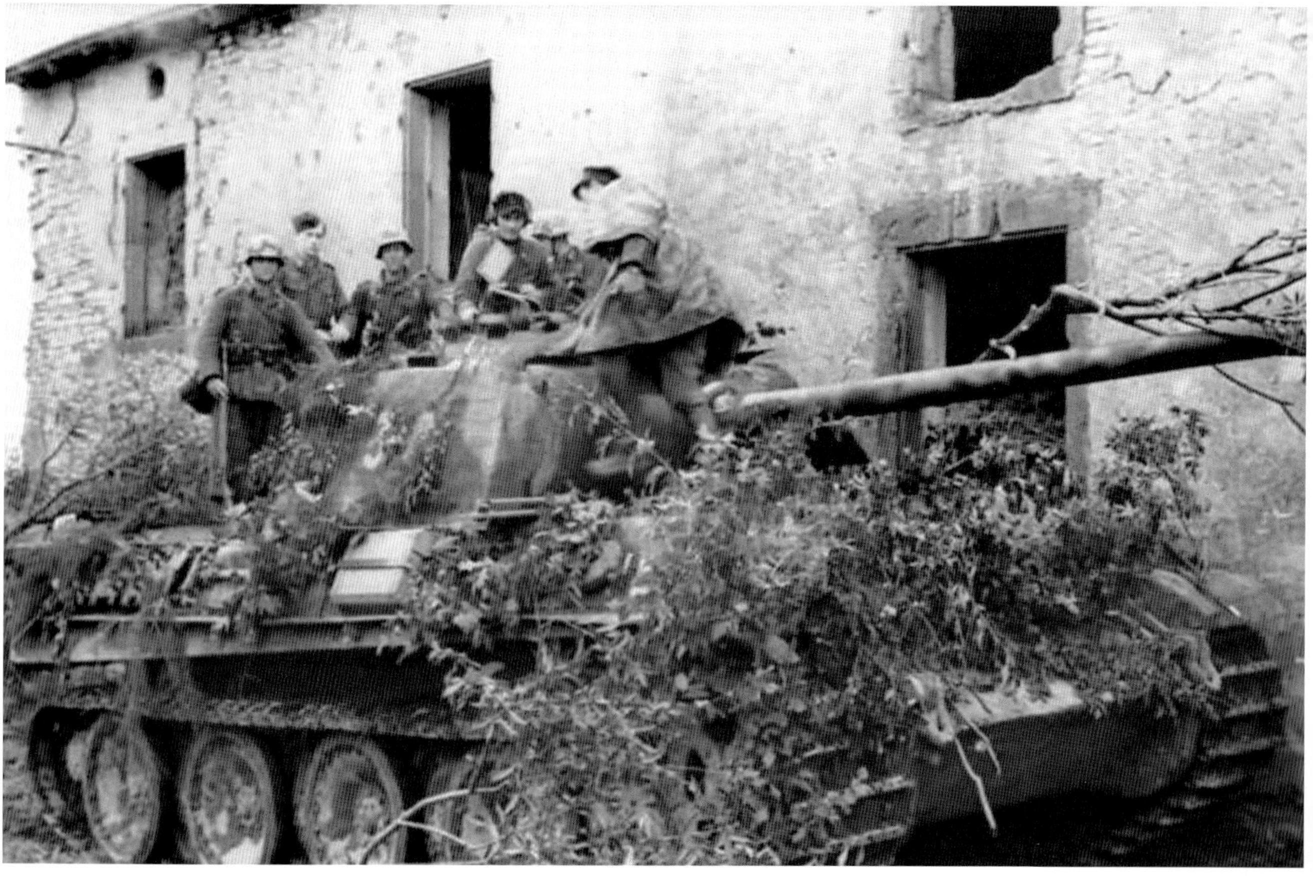

(**Opposite, above**) Panzergrenadiers are seen dismounting from an Sd.Kfz.251/1 Ausf.C and going into action. The Ausf.C is identified by the shape of the cowls on the side of the engine compartment. Note the summer camouflage scheme of dark yellow with a heavily over-sprayed mottle pattern of olive green.

(**Opposite, below**) A common occurrence during the second half of the war period, grenadiers hitching a lift onboard a Panther Ausf.G in France. Saplings have been applied over the Panther including some large branches in order to help conceal it for enemy observation. The Panzer has purposely halted next to a building to avoid Allied detection.

(**Above**) Hitlerjugend troops belonging to the infamous 12 SS-Panzer-Division HJ can be seen operating against British forces in a field. By mid-July 1944 both the regular and Waffen-SS divisions were fighting for survival.

An 8.8cm FlaK gun during a fire mission against Allied aerial attacks. These FlaK guns were constantly engaging aerial targets during the last year of the war and the crews worked intensely at serving their pieces in order to try and defend the skies.

(**Opposite**) Two photographs show a StuG.III Ausf.G with an extensive covering of zimmerit anti-magnetic mine paste and an interesting camouflage scheme on the side skirts or Schurzen. Note the second photo with the assault gun crossing a shallow river and showing the unit insignia on the rear superstructure plate, which is unfortunately difficult to identify. Due to the long distances the grenadiers had to march, it was common to hitch a lift on board various modes of transport in order to bring them or withdraw them from the battlefield quickly and effectively.

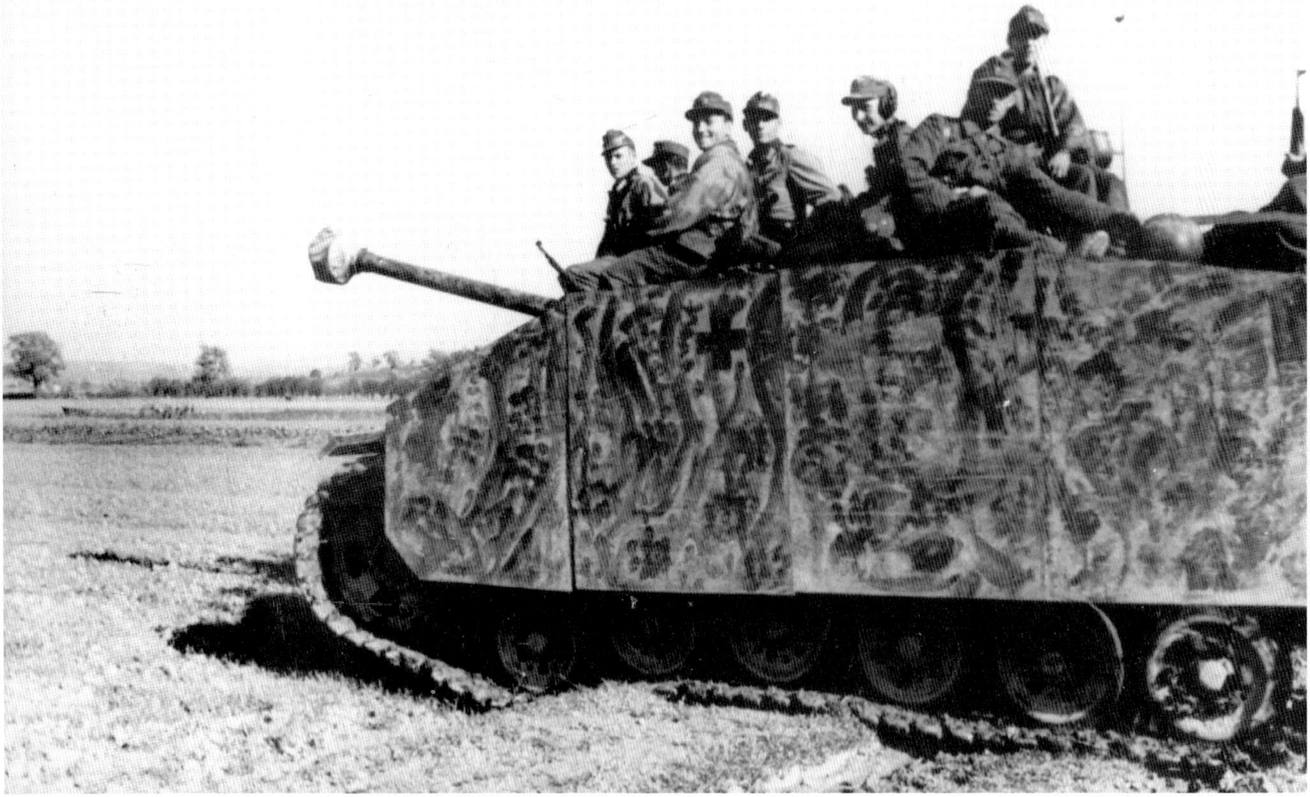

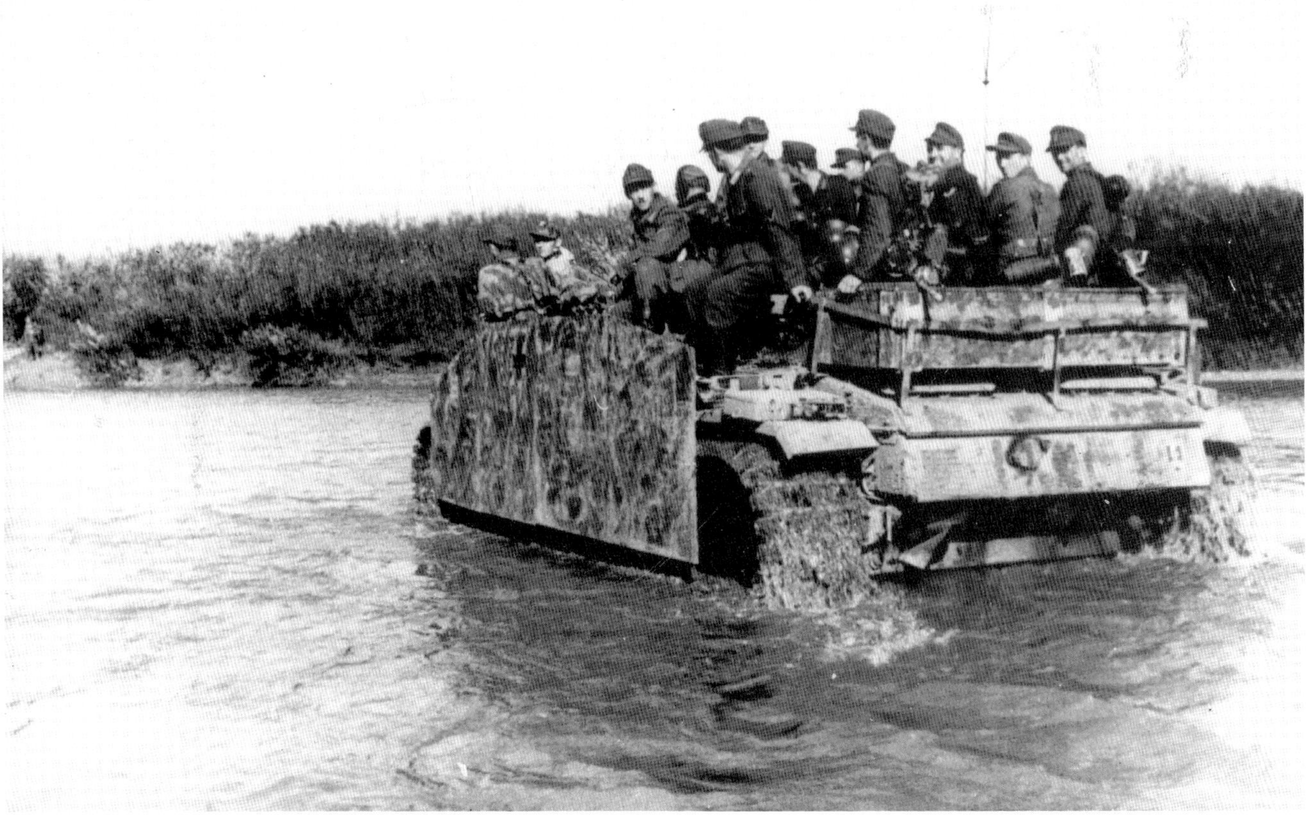

(**Above**) Wehrmacht troops can be seen making a hasty retreat from a burning building during operations in France. The NCO at the front appears to be armed with an MP40 machine pistol, while the soldier following behind carries the standard infantryman's bolt action rifle, the Karabiner 98K.

(**Opposite, above**) A photograph taken from onboard a Panther medium tank showing its commander looking down upon the crew of a Sd.Kfz.251/1 Ausf.D. The vehicle has camouflage netting attached and foliage could be easily threaded into it. This Ausf.D mounts an MG42 machine gun complete with gun shield.

(**Opposite, below**) This 8.8cm FlaK 36 or FlaK 37 has been caught by the photographer the moment the gun is fired in anger against an enemy target. The soldiers in the foreground still have their ears covered against the sound of the gun blast, while one of the ammunition handlers can be seen with one of the projectiles on his shoulder preparing to reload the piece.

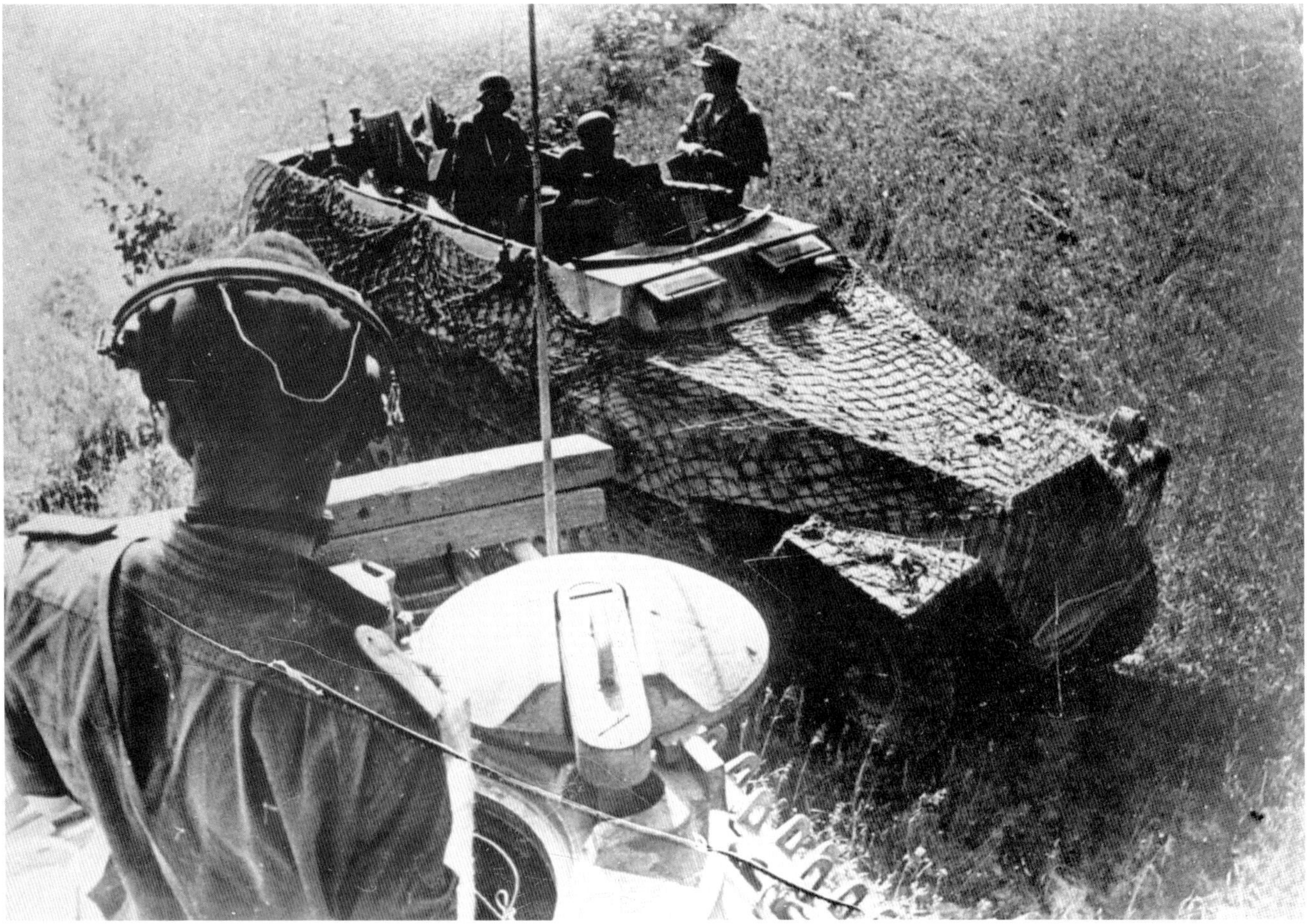

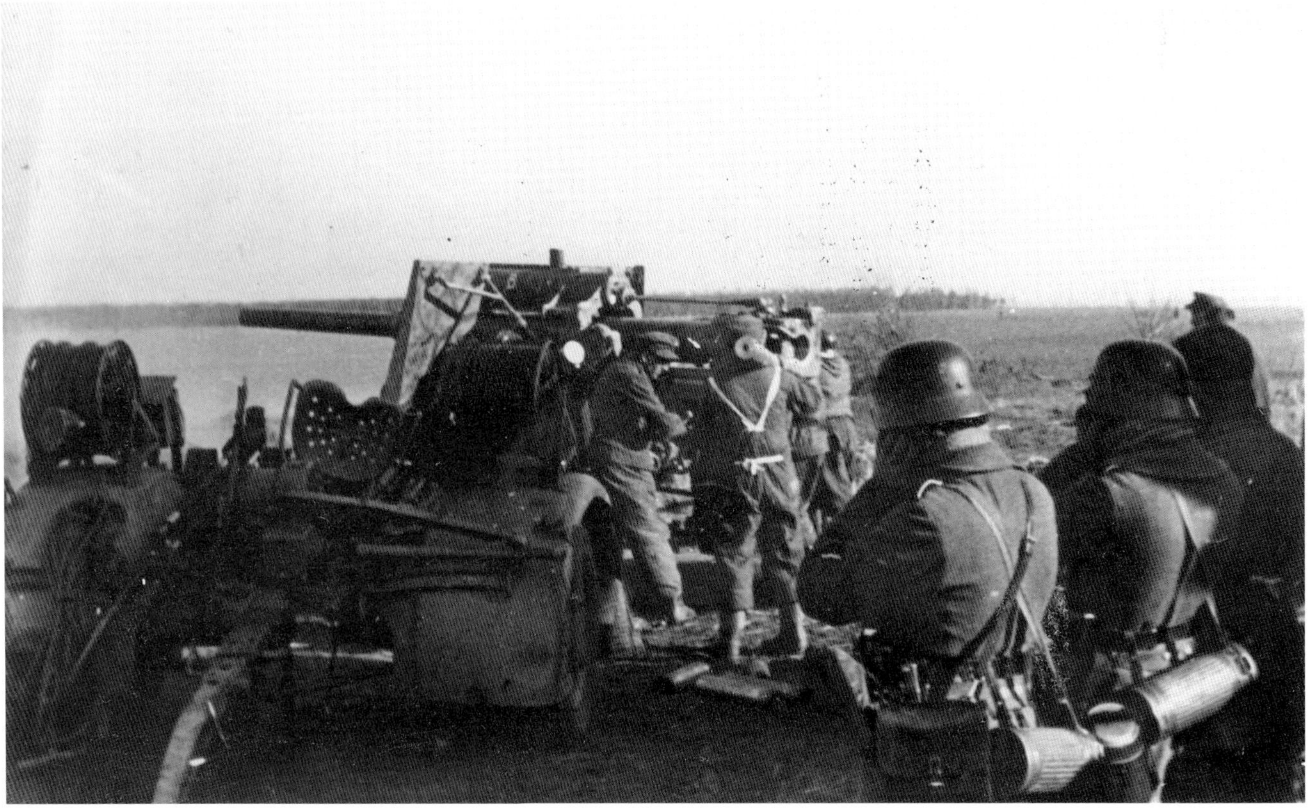

(**Above**) An Sd.Kfz.251 halftrack follows a late variant Panzerkampfwagen IV towards the battlefront. Extensive foliage covers the halftrack in order to try and conceal it against both ground and aerial observation.

(**Opposite, above**) A Mittlerer Zugkraftwagen prime mover hauls a 8.8cm FlaK gun towards the battlefront. These halftracks were widely used during the war, not only to tow FlaK guns, but 10cm sK 18 and 15cm sFH 18 artillery as well. They were regarded by both the Heer and Waffen-SS as the workhorse halftrack of the Second World War.

(**Opposite, below**) Tiger 323 from the 3/s SS-Panzer-Abteilung 101 makes its way to the front in Normandy on 7 June 1944, with SS-Hauptscharführer Barkhausen in the commander's cupola.

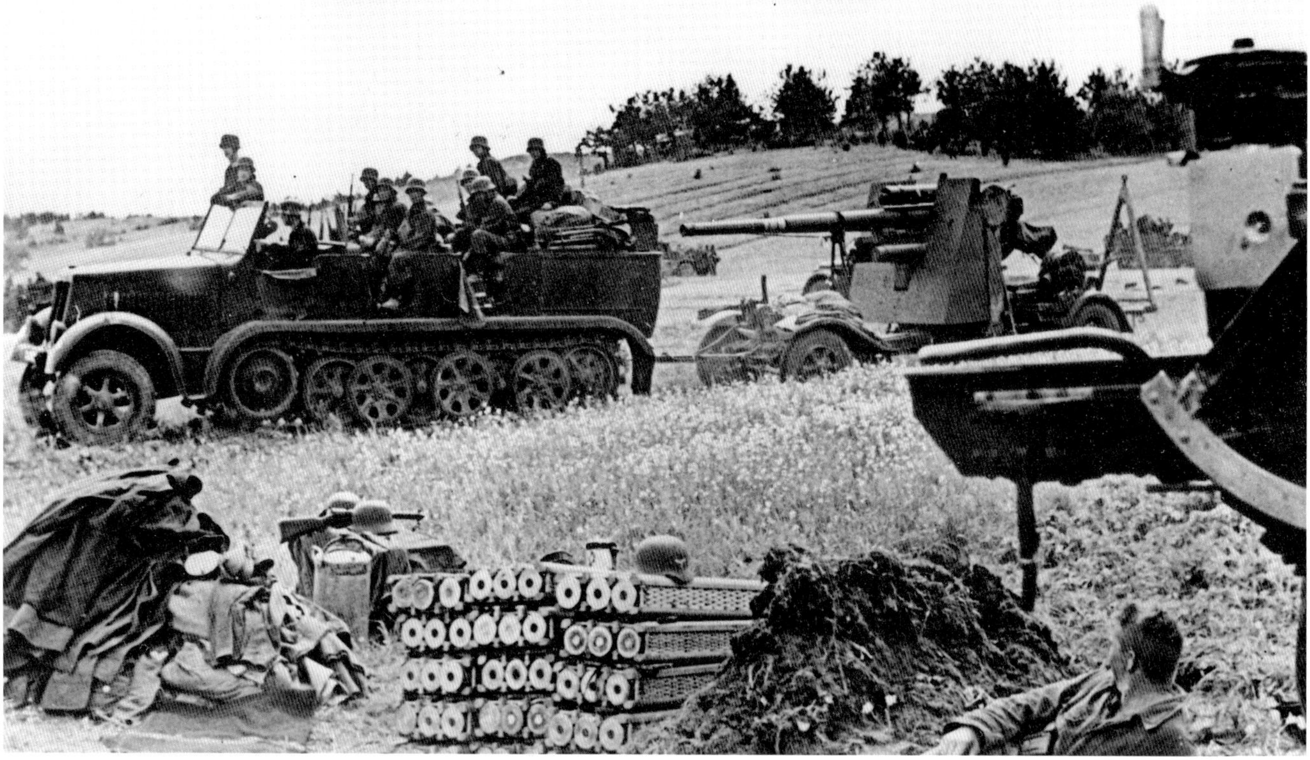

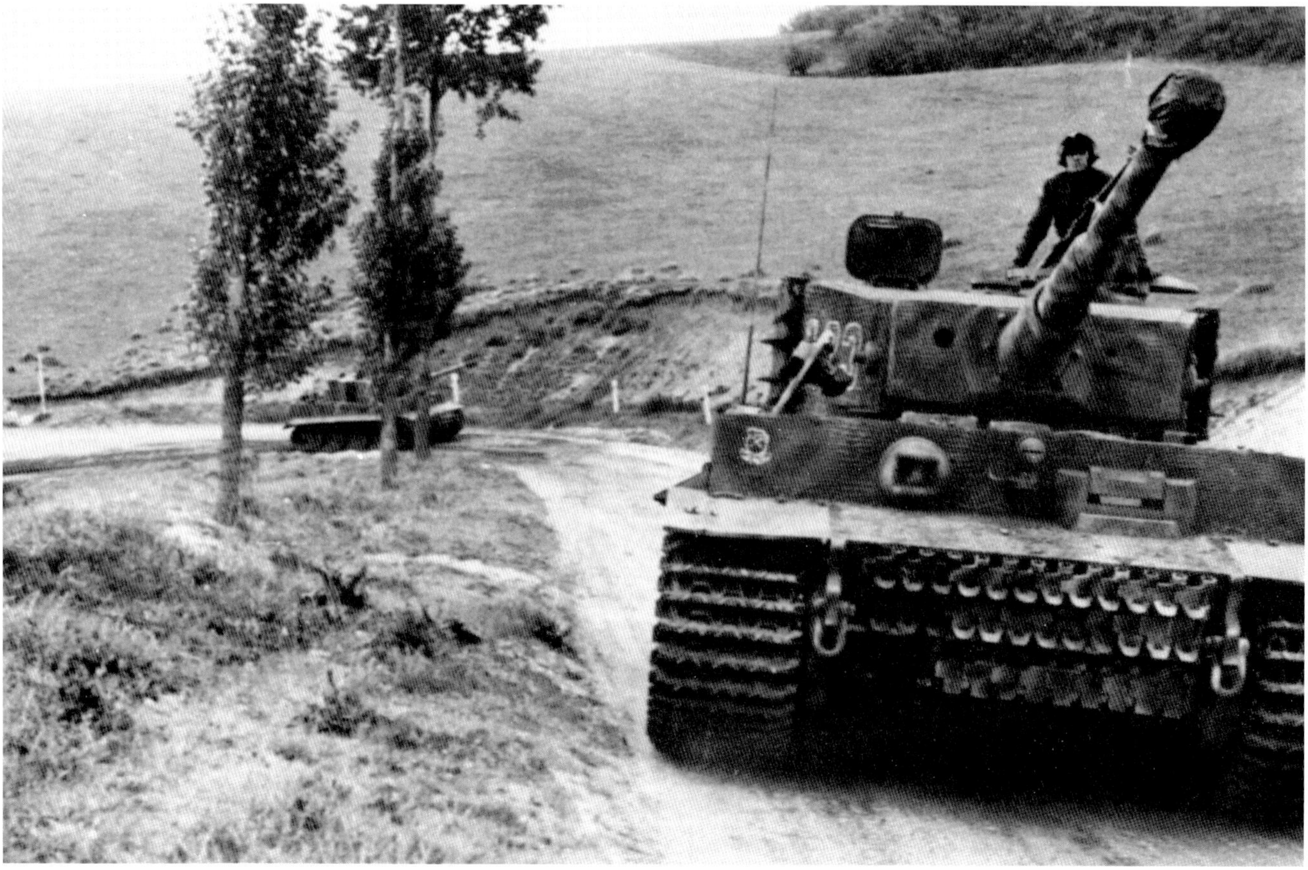

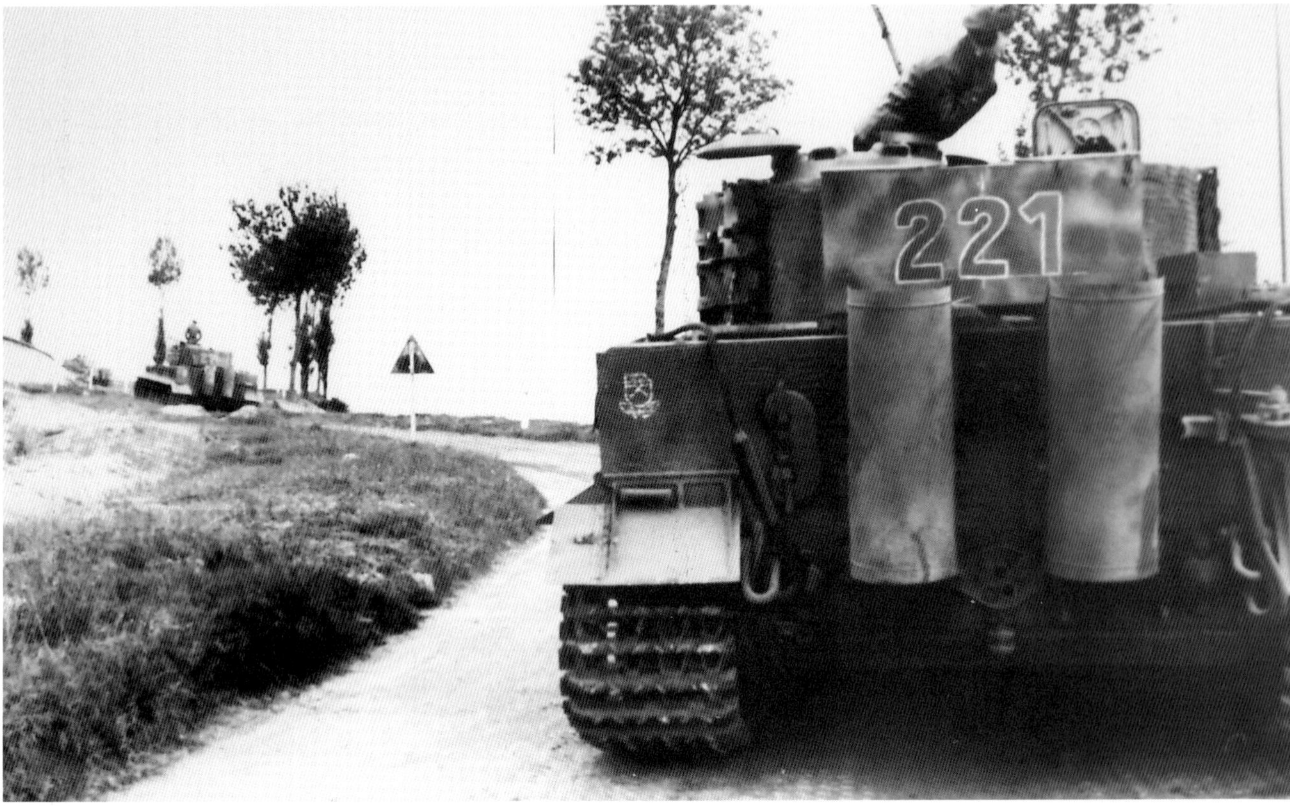
221

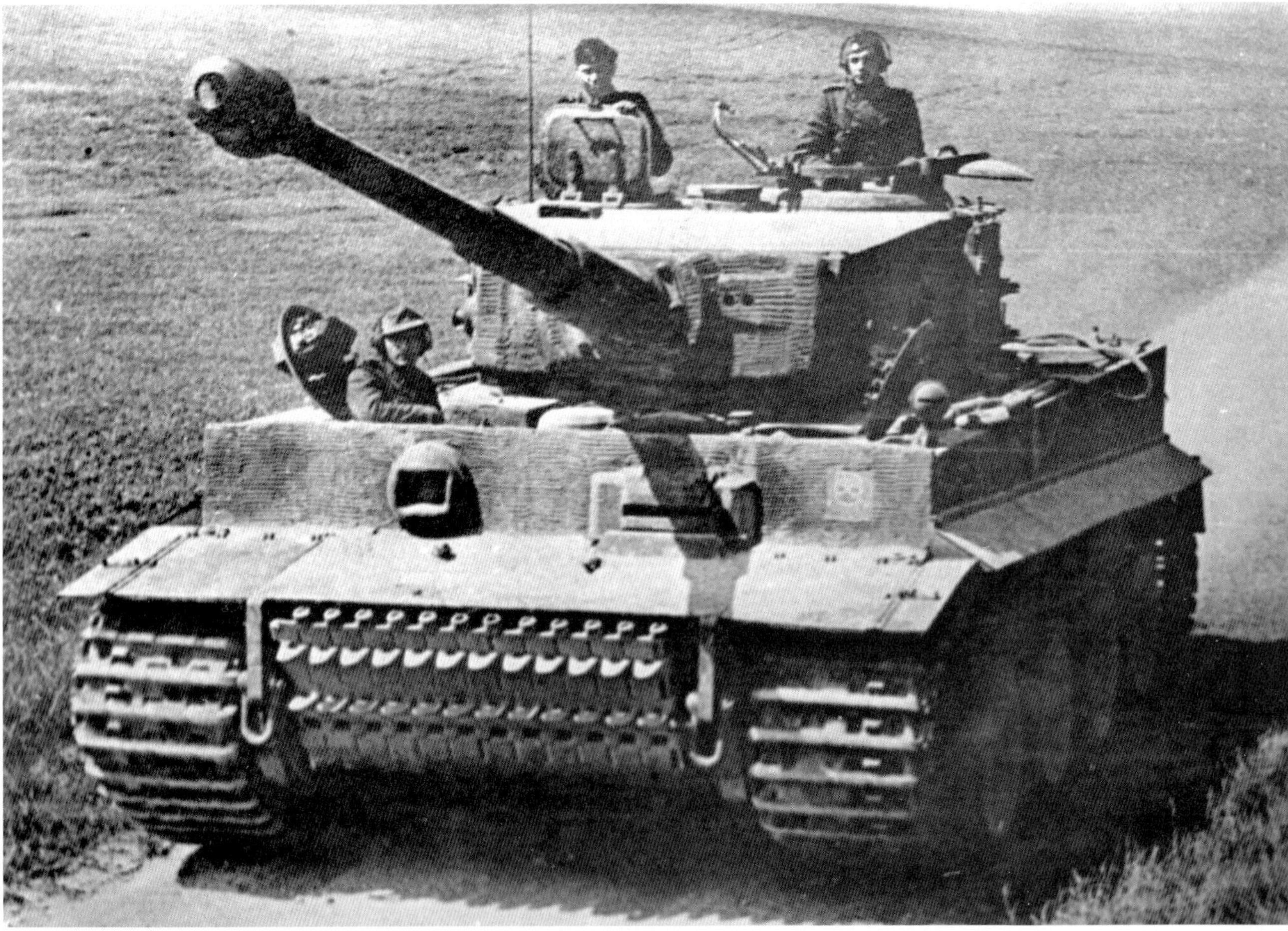

(**Opposite, above**) Tiger 221 from SS-Panzer-Abteilung 101 can be seen negotiating a road in northern France. The Leibstandarte (LSSAH) SS Panzer Corps had been reformed in early July 1944 which comprised of the 12th SS Panzer-Division Hitlerjugend. The LSSAH had been in a holding position north of the River Seine prior to the Normandy invasion to counter a possible landing in the Pas de Calais area, so the first units did not arrive in the Normandy sector until the night of 27 June, with the whole division taking another week to arrive.

(**Above**) An interesting photograph showing Tiger tank 205 of SS-Panzer-Abteilung 101 on the advance en route to Morgny. Panzer ace SS-Hauptsturmführer Michael Wittmann can be seen standing in the turret. By early August 1944 Wittmann would be killed in an ambush which resulted in his tank being blown up, killing him and all his crew near the town of Saint-Aignan-de-Cramesnil.

(**Opposite, below**) Another view of the Tiger tank rolling along a road in Normandy. During the war 1354 Tiger Is were constructed. In spite of the military reversal on both the Western and Eastern Fronts, these vehicles constantly demonstrated both the lethalness of their 8.8cm guns and their invulnerability against Allied anti-tank shells.

(**Above**) Soldiers of the 12 SS-Panzer-Division Hitlerjugend take cover during extensive fighting in Normandy. The position here comprises a 7.5cm leichtes Infanteriegeshütz 18 field gun placed overlooking open terrain. This particular weapon was used in direct infantry support. The gun was very versatile in combat and the crew often aggressively positioned it which usually meant the piece was regularly exposed on the battlefield, as seen here.

(**Opposite, above**) As a column of vehicles and troops march on a road, a well emplaced 2cm FlaK gun can be seen defending the column from a possible attack. This weapon had an effective ceiling and vertical range of 2,200 metres against a target. The gun had a cycle rate of fire of 280rpm, and a practical rate of 120rpm.

(**Opposite, below**) A well sighted elevated 2cm FlaK gun during a fire mission against enemy aerial activity. The gunner sits in the gunner's chair. The gun is attached to its Sd.Ah.51 trailer, which is propped up on its integral landing skid. In this position the gun could be fired in an emergency.

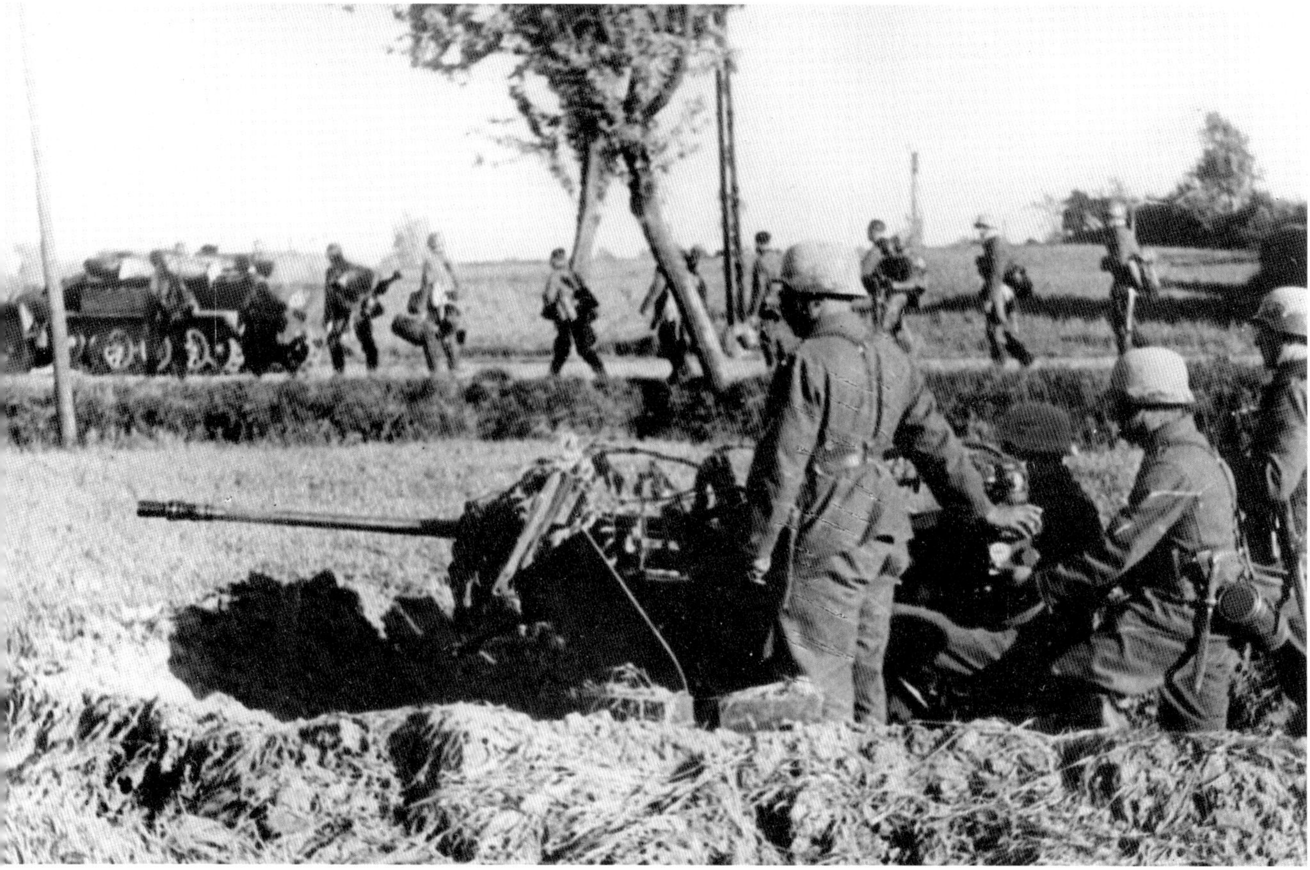

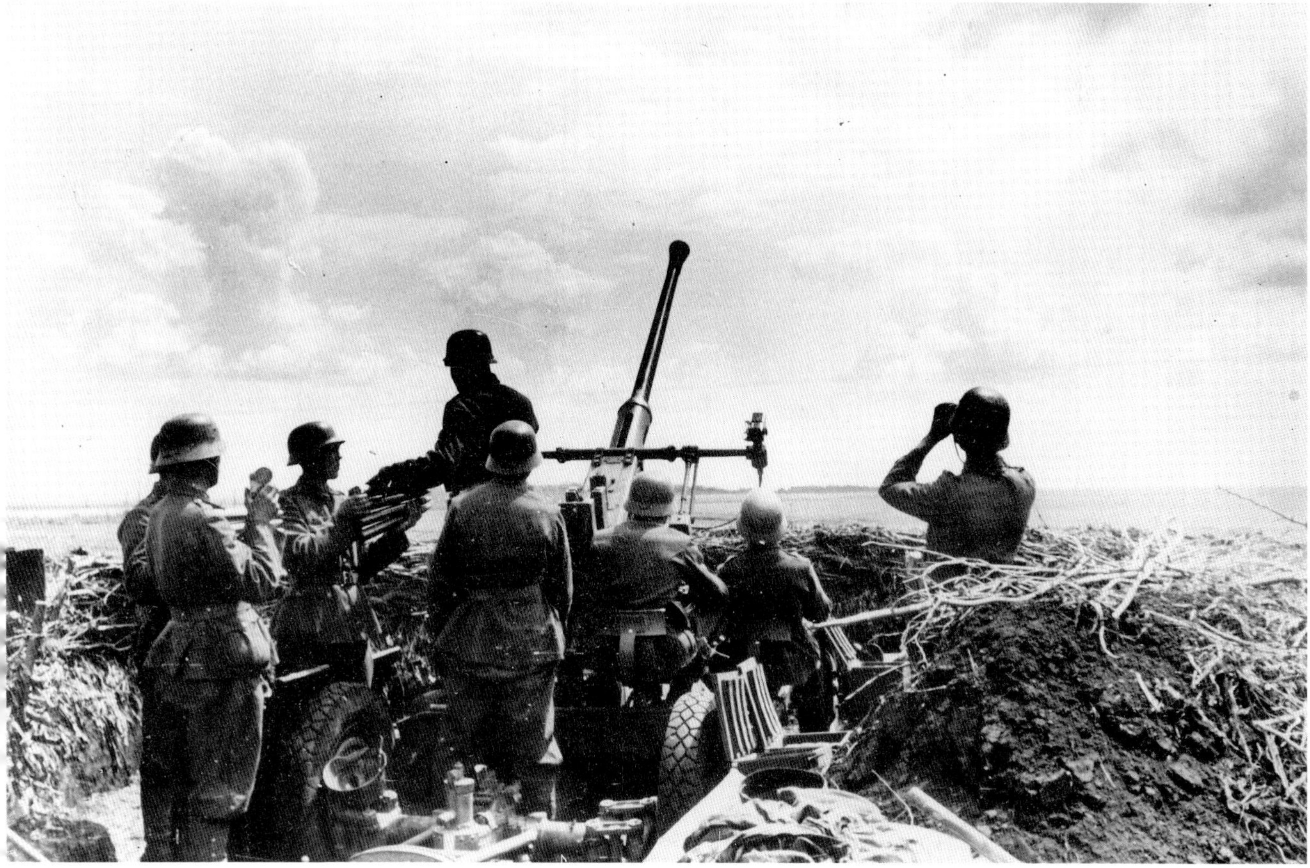

Paratroopers or Fallschirmjäger mortar crew with their 8cm Granatwerfer 34 mortar in a dugout during a fire mission. It was normally very common for infantry, especially during intensive long periods of action, to fire their mortar from either trenches or dug-in positions where the mortar crew could also be protected from enemy fire.

Out in the field is a 15cm Nebelwerfer 41. These six barreled rocket launchers served with units of the Nebel-truppen to deliver high-explosives into the enemy lines. For firing, an electrical cable led to the remote firing mechanism running from a junction box between two launch tubes. The firer then could safely fire the weapon from a distance without getting hit by the back blast. Note some of the projectiles laying near to the piece ready for firing. A well concealed prime mover has transported the rockets and the troops are seen unloading them.

What appears to be a Luftwaffe crew manning a dug-in and camouflaged 2cm FlaK 38. Anti-aircraft guns were typically deployed in defence roles, defending areas such as main roads and bridges in order to ward off enemy air attacks aimed at harassing the movement of troops, weapons and supplies.

A motorcycle combination complete with MG42 advances along a road. Behind are a column of type 166 Schwimmwagen amphibious cars.

(**Above**) A number of Wehrmacht troops are on the march in France. These soldiers carry standard infantrymen equipment. Among them is an MG34 machine gun team, with the gunner carrying his weapon on his shoulder.

(**Opposite**) An SS soldier holding the rank of an SS-Rottenführer is seen perched from the sunroof of a civilian vehicle being used for combat. The car carries a summer camouflage scheme of green and red patches over a sand base colour. Some foliage is attached to the vehicle in order to break up its distinctive shape.

(**Below**) A Volkswagen Kübelwagen is stationary on the side of the road with troops conversing. On the road a column of support vehicles are burning, more than likely attacked by an enemy aircraft. In northern France the Germans found movement by road during the day perilous, and columns of vehicles were exposed to constant attacks. It therefore led to many units moving at night, or through wooded or forested areas.

During a fire mission and this 8.8cm FlaK gun can be seen in action against an enemy ground target. Note the kill rings painted along the barrel, denoting its successful engagements against ground and aerial targets.

A Luftwaffe FlaK gunner is seen here loading his projectile into the breech of his 8.8cm FlaK gun. It appears that much of the gun has been concealed with foliage in order to break up its distinctive shape from ground or aerial observation.

An unusual photograph showing what appears to be a Luftwaffe FlaK crew undressed down to their underwear preparing their 8.8cm weapon for a fire mission, as all the personnel are wearing their steel helmets.

Sitting on the tracks of a Sturmgeschütz, the StuG crew can be seen conversing in the field. They wear the now familiar assault gun uniform which was similar cut to that of their Panzertruppen counterparts. This special field-grey uniform was worn by all crews of tank destroyer and self-propelled assault gun units. Note in the centre of the photograph an Sd.Kfz.250 Ausf.A. In the far distance is a StuG.III Ausf.G.

(**Above**) A close-up view of a dirty-faced motorcyclist. The soldier is wearing the motorcycle waterproof coat which was a double-breasted rubberized item of clothing. It was made of cotton twill coated rubber with watertight seams and the coat was worn over the service uniform. The coat was loose fitting and the ends of the garment could be easily gathered in around the wearer's legs and buttoned into position which allowed easier and safer movement while riding the motorcycle. The motorcycle coat was grey-green in colour and had a woollen field-grey material collar with large pockets. When in use the wearer normally wore the standard issue army canvas and leather gloves or mittens. Normal leather army boots were often worn.

(**Opposite, above**) A Panther Ausf.G rolls through a French town in the summer of 1944. The Panzer has extensive foliage attached to break up the distinctive shape and an interesting camouflage scheme applied comprising a base colour of dark yellow and olive green patches and spots.

(**Opposite, below**) A FlaK crew preparing their weapon for a fire mission during defensive measures in the summer of 1944. Although German FlaK and field commanders were fully aware of the fruitless attempts by its forces to establish a cohesive defensive line, the troops followed instructions implicitly in a number of areas to halt the Allied drive. Again and again the FlaK units fought to stave off both ground and aerial attacks. However, the lack of fuel, spare parts, ammunition stocks and weapons, coupled with the lack of trained crews all played a major part in reducing the effectiveness of the FlaK and field divisions in the final year of the war.

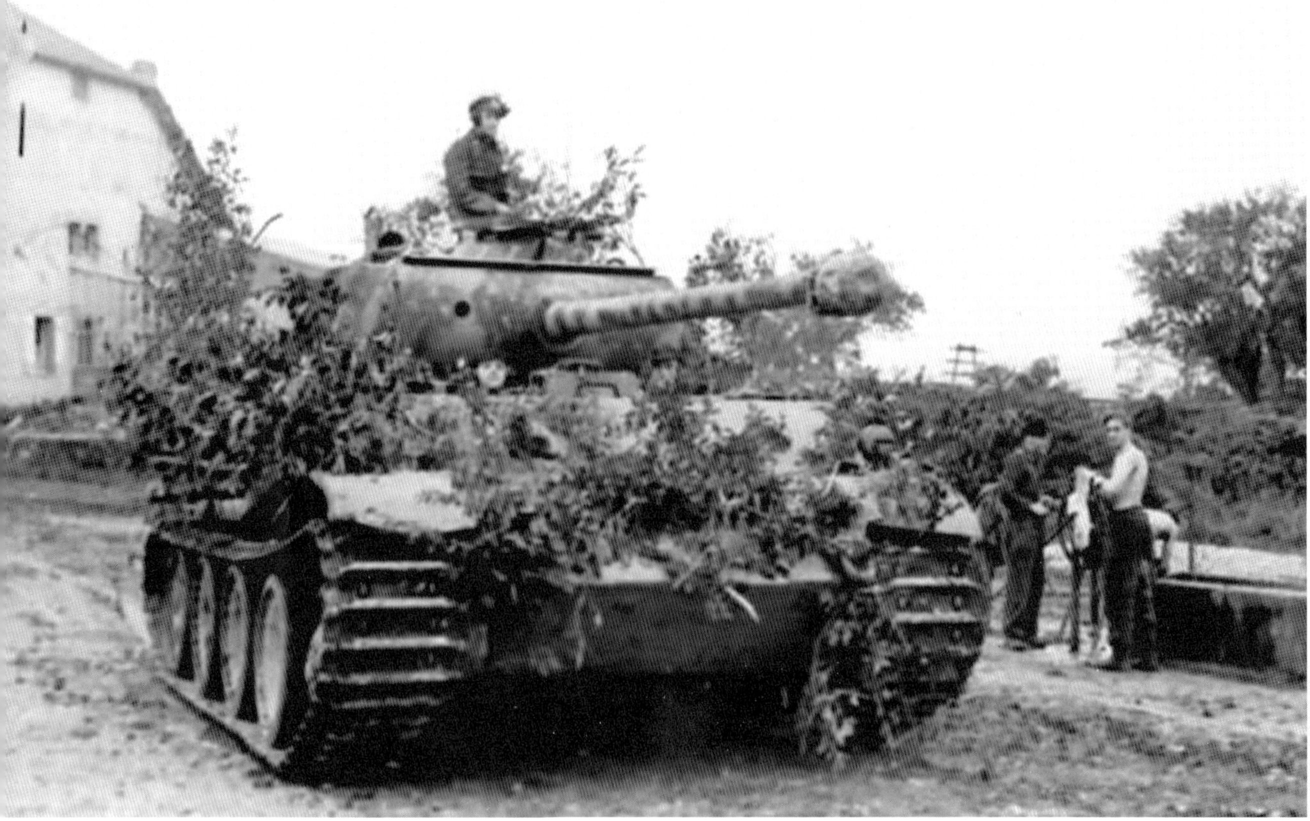

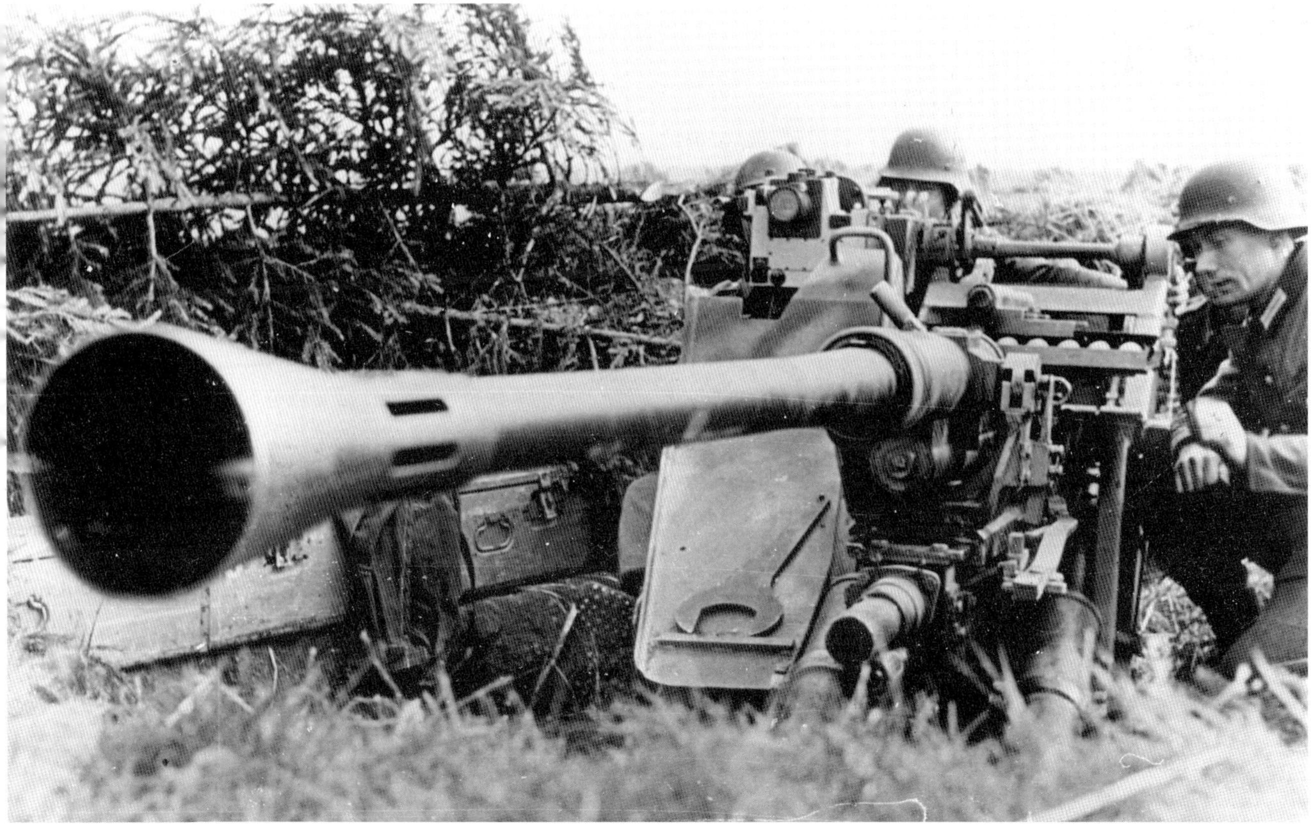

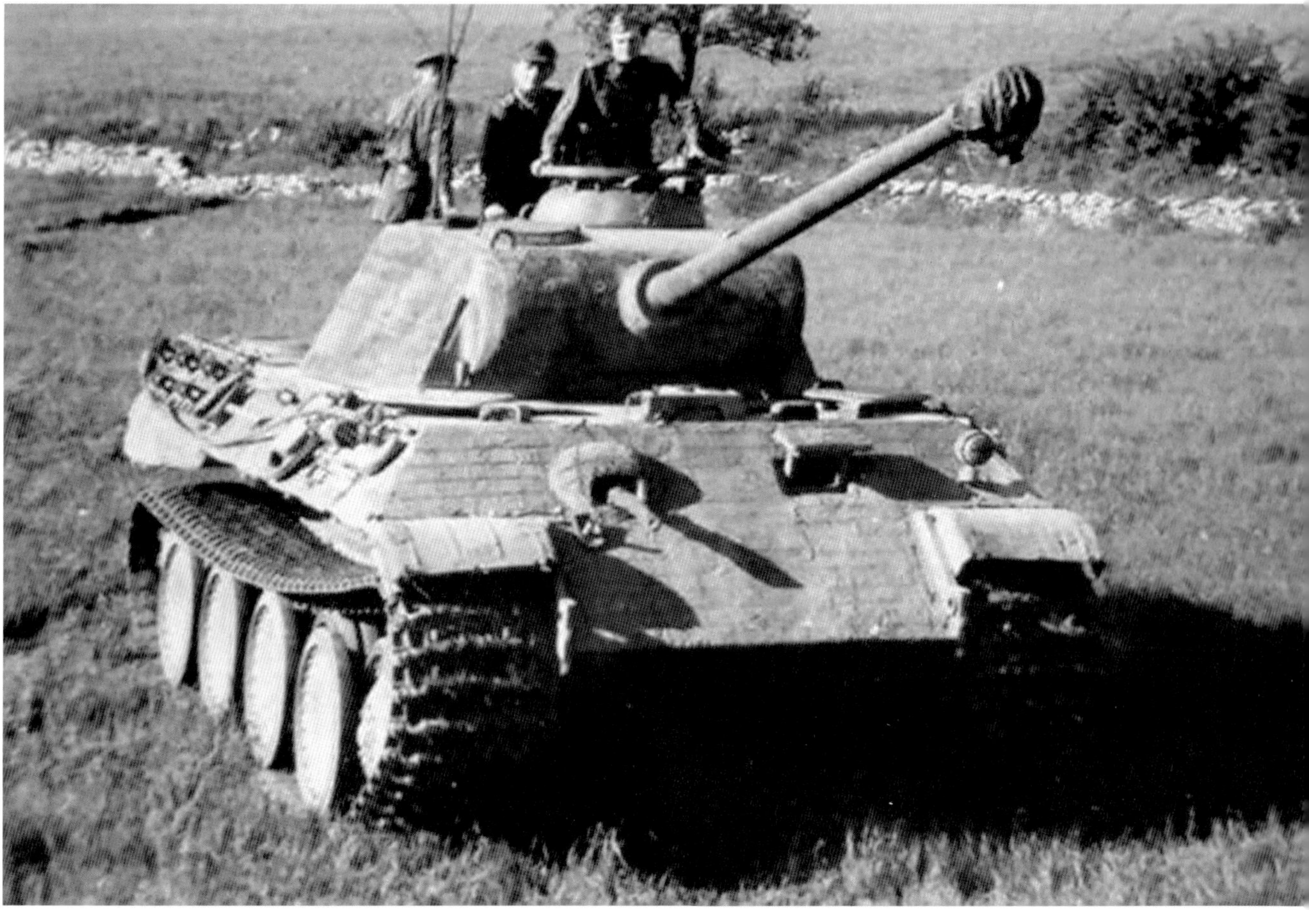

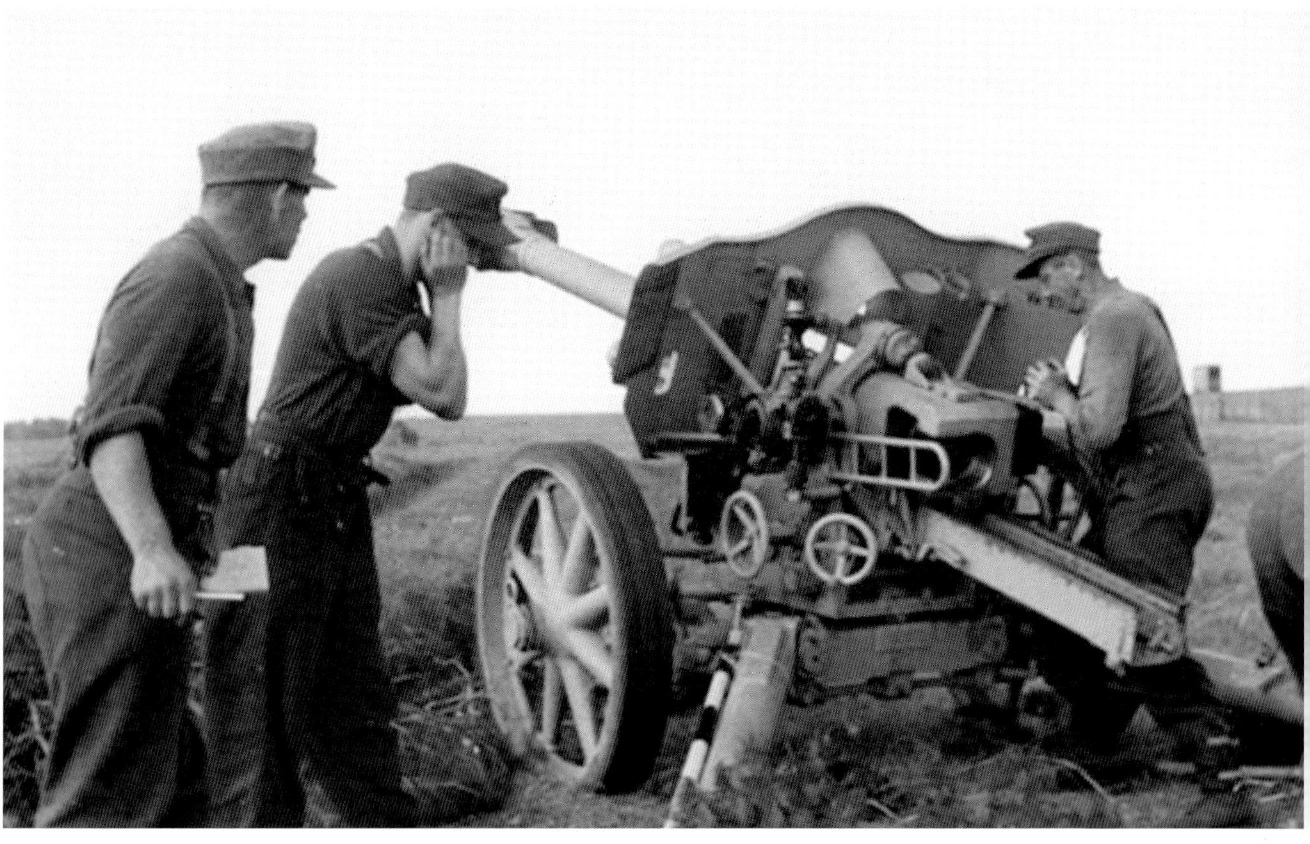

A Fallschirmjäger 8cm Granatwerfer 34 mortar and crew in the process of firing a projectile against an enemy target. There was a platoon of four 8cm mortars assigned to a grenadier battalion's machine gun company. The Germans found the mortar so effective that they often used many captured Soviet mortars and fired their own ammunition from them using German firing tables.

(**Opposite, above**) A Panther tank advancing across a field during operations in France in the summer of 1944. This vehicle belongs to the SS Das Reich Division. In June 1944 there were initially only two Panther-equipped Panzer regiments on the Western Front, with a total of 156 Panthers between them. From June through August 1944, an additional seven Panther regiments were sent into France, which increased the strength to 432 Panthers.

(**Opposite, below**) A Wehrmacht 10.5cm le FH 18/42 infantry gun crew in action during a fire mission. The 10.5cm gun provided both the Wehrmacht and Waffen-SS with a versatile, relatively mobile base of fire.

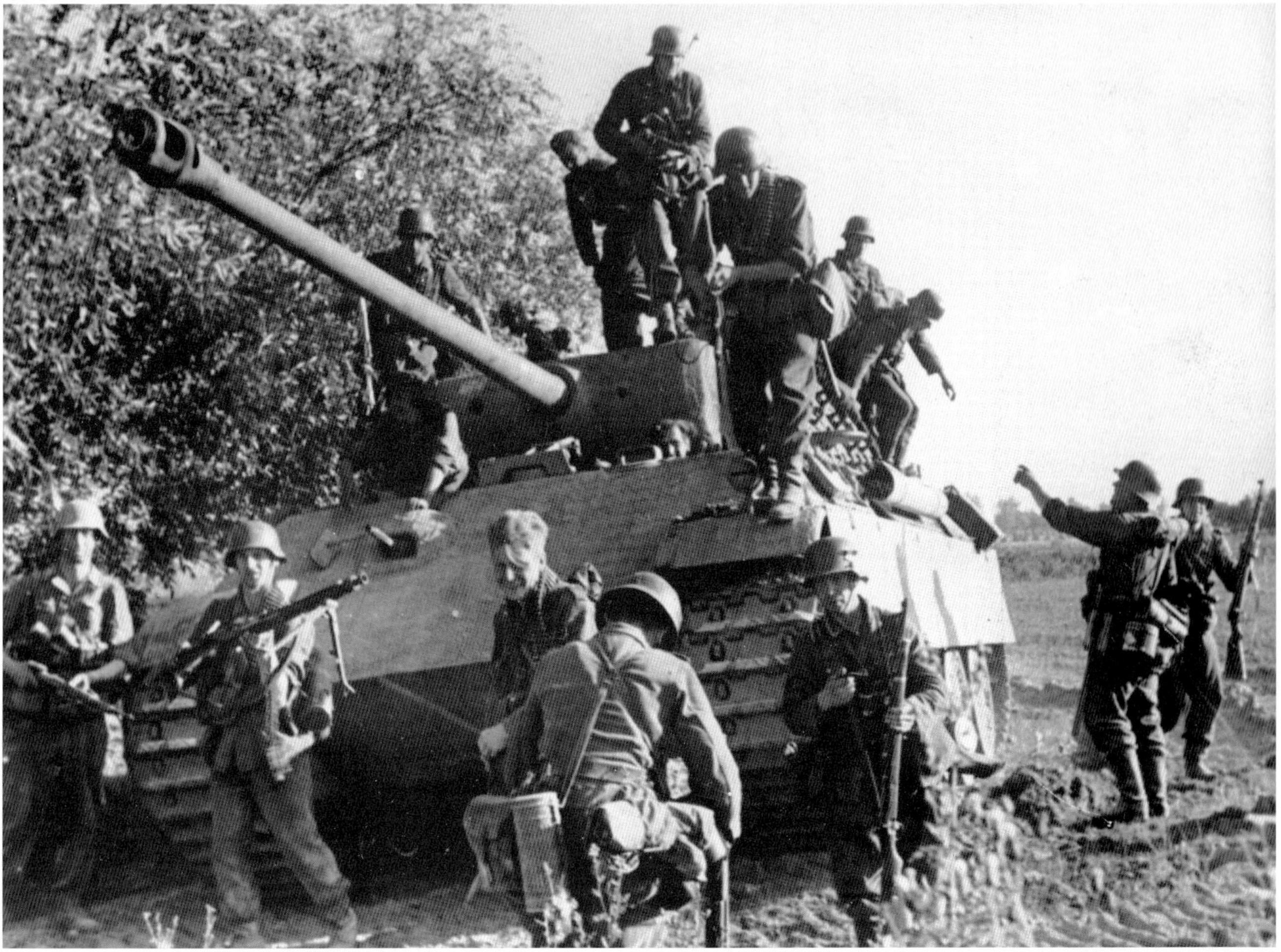

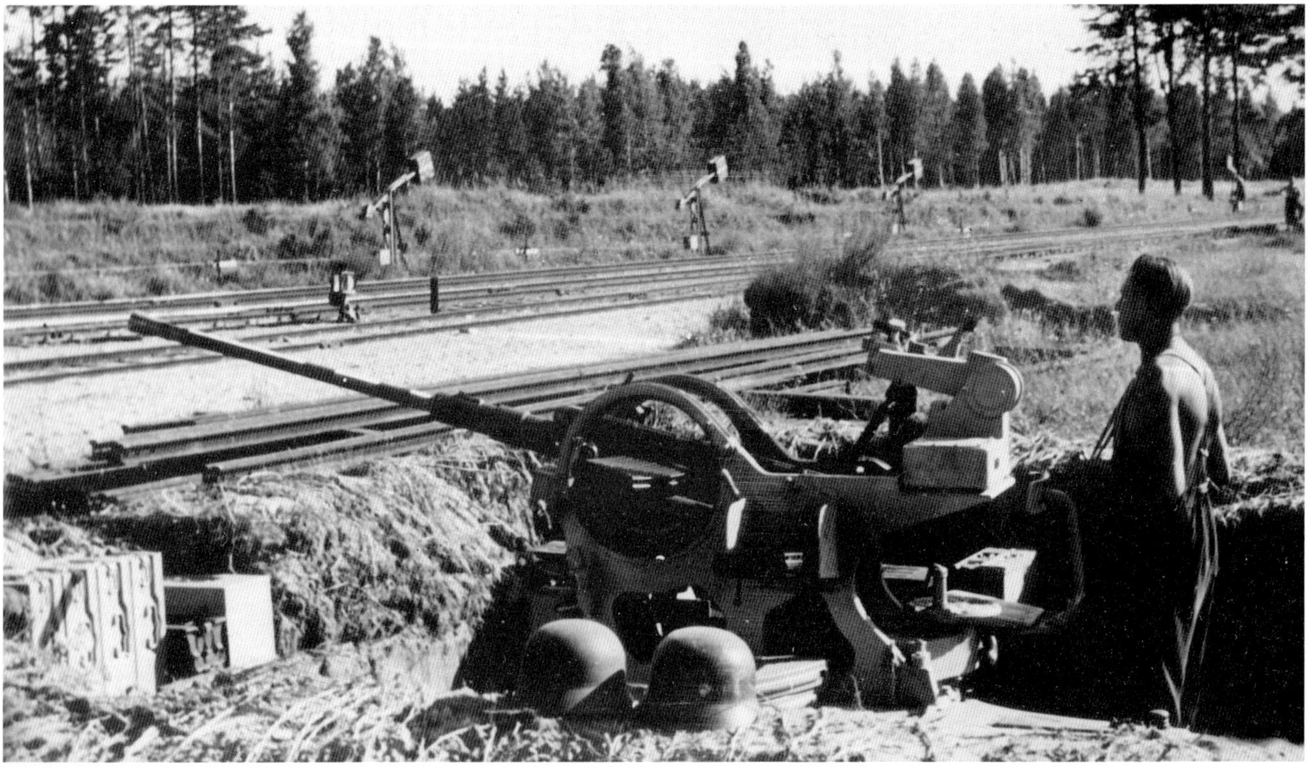

(**Opposite, above**) Part of an infantry section, including their MG42 machine gun team, dismount from a Panther Ausf.G. This early variant still retains Zimmerit anti-magnetic mine paste. The vehicle has no visible markings.

(**Above**) A photograph taken at the moment a Nebeltruppe battery is about to launch its deadly Nebelwerfer rockets against an enemy position. Because the weapon was too dangerous for the crew to remain close to the launcher while the piece was being fired, it was fired remotely using an electrical detonator attached to a cable, which ran to the piece. Note how the battery of men are quickly withdrawing from their weapon after the piece has been loaded for firing.

(**Opposite, below**) An emplaced 2cm FlaK gun affords an excellent view of the details of the mount and turntable. This weapon has been purposely positioned near a rail line in order to defend it from aerial attacks.

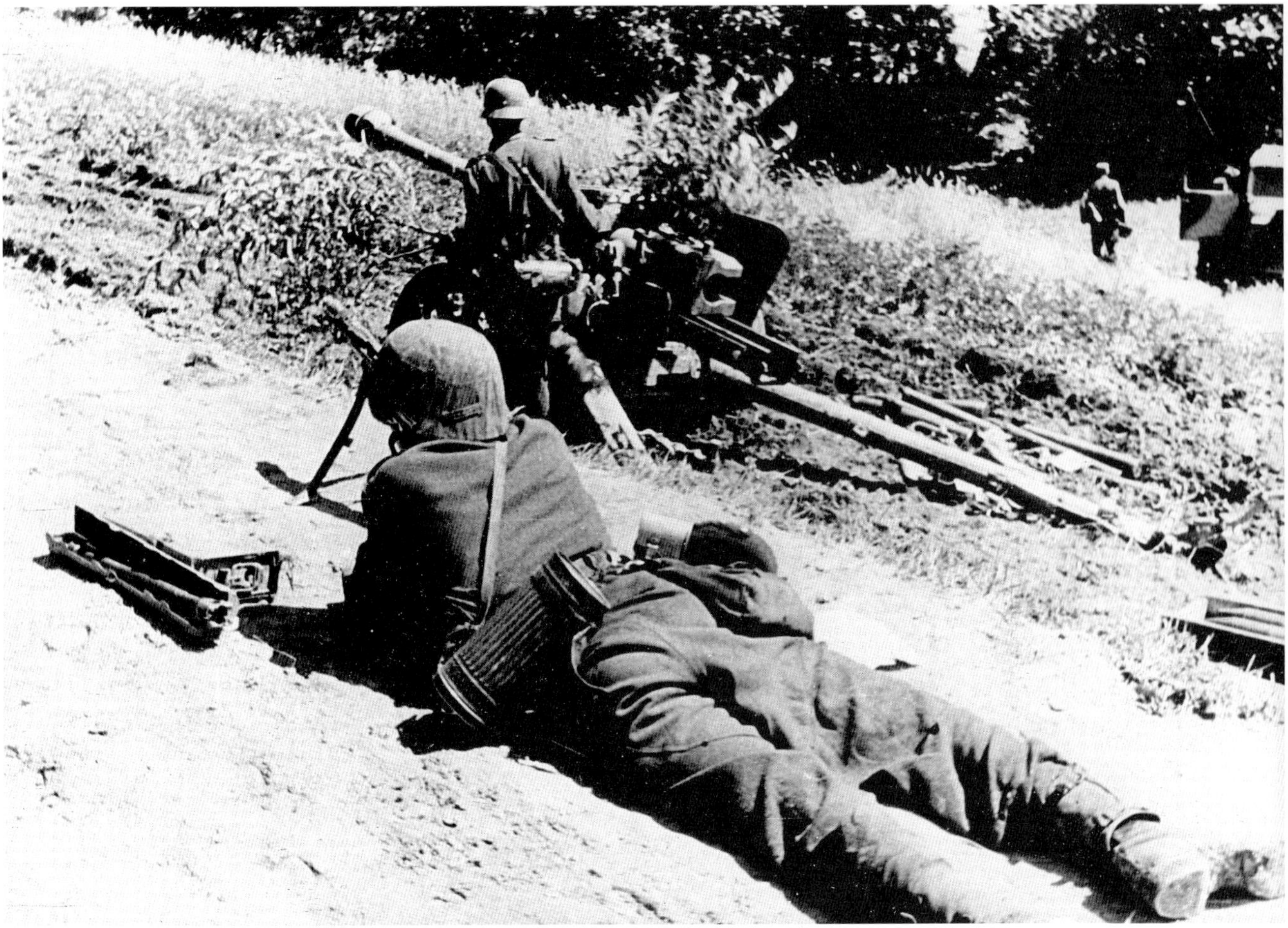

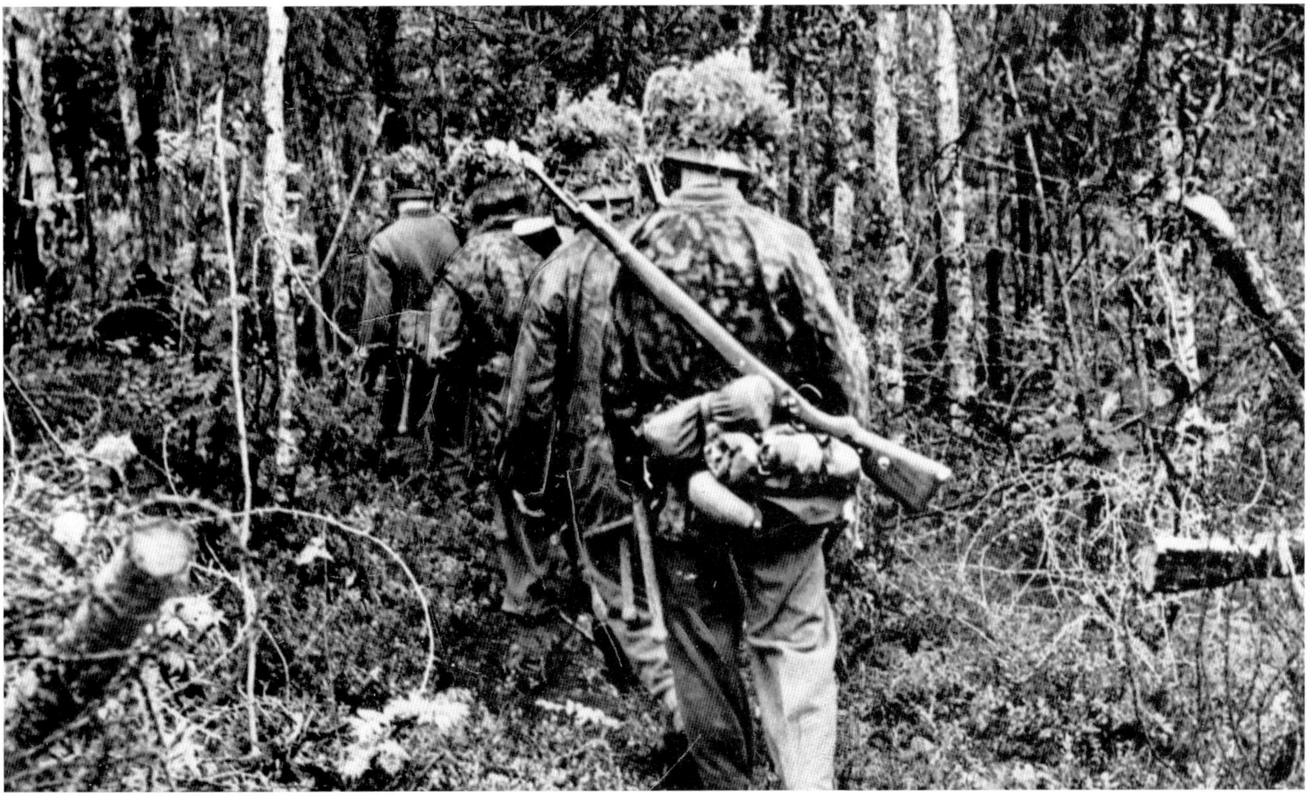

(**Opposite, above**) Defending a road, a PaK gun and an MG34 light machine gunner prepares to engage the enemy.

(**Opposite, below**) Waffen-SS soldiers advance through a wooded area. Their summer camouflage smocks blend well with the local terrain and afford additional concealment during daylight movement.

(**Above**) Here in this photograph a Marder I tank destroyer or Panzerjäger can be seen in France in 1944. This vehicle mounted a 7.5cm PaK 40 anti-tank gun. The majority of these tank destroyers were built on the base of the Lorraine French artillery tractor which the Germans acquired in 1940. The Marder I became a significant component of the armoured fighting vehicles of the reformed 21st Panzer Division in Normandy.

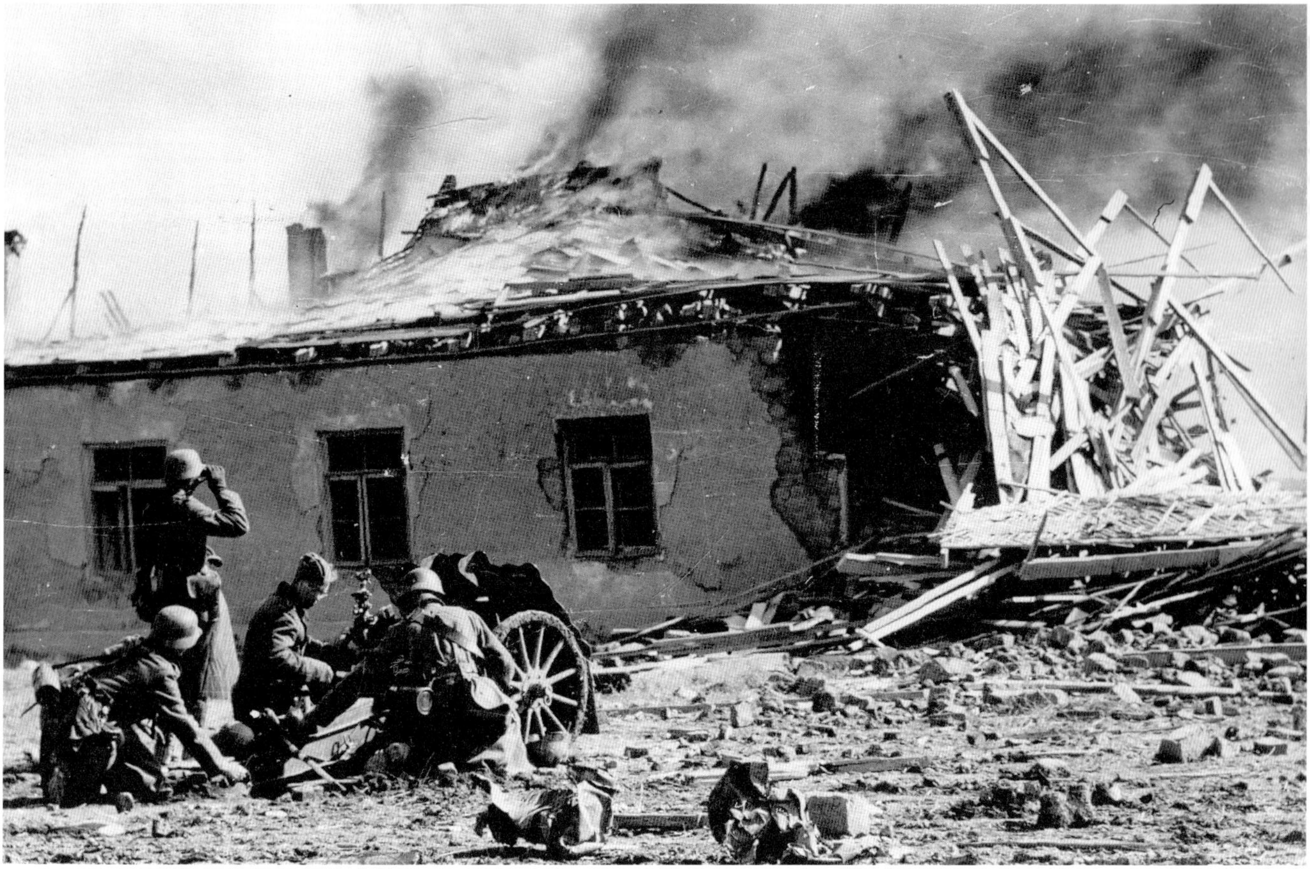

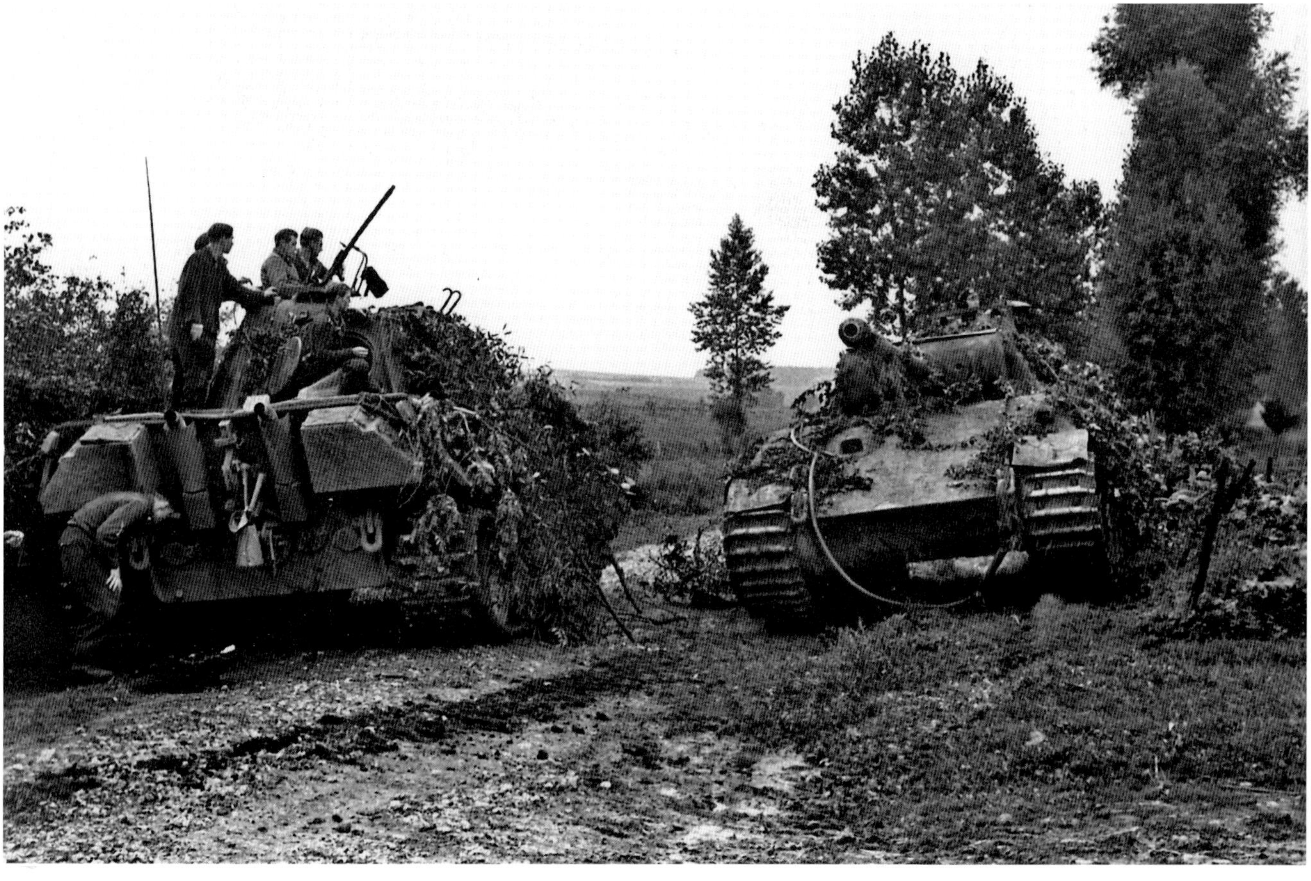

(**Opposite, above**) Positioned next to a damaged building is a 7.5cm leichtes Infanteriegeschütz 18. This particular weapon was used in direct infantry support. The gun was very versatile in combat and the crew often aggressively positioned it, which usually meant the piece was regularly exposed on the battlefield.

(**Above**) Troops withdrawing along a dirt road by animal draught. Much of the components that made up the infantry and grenadier divisions in 1944 had horse drawn transport as their main mode of moving supplies from one part of the front to another.

(**Opposite, below**) Two Panthers can be seen out in the field in the summer of 1944. Both Panthers have extensive camouflage attached to the vehicle. By 1944 the disparity of armoured vehicles meant that Panzers like the Panther had to wage continuous defensive battles in order to wear down the enemy in a war of attrition.

(**Above**) French civilians inside a village pose for the camera sitting on an abandoned Jagdpanzer 38. The Jagdpanzer was designed, produced and fielded as a result of an interruption in StuG.III Ausf.G production, due to an Allied air raid on its production plant. These were stop gap tank hunters.

(**Opposite**) Two photographs showing knocked out Tiger tanks in the Falaise Pocket. The Battle of the Falaise Pocket ended the Battle of Normandy with a decisive German defeat with more than forty German divisions destroyed during the battle of Normandy. Hundreds of German tanks and armoured vehicles were destroyed at Falaise which led to surviving German units retreating through France over the Seine River in order to avoid complete annihilation.

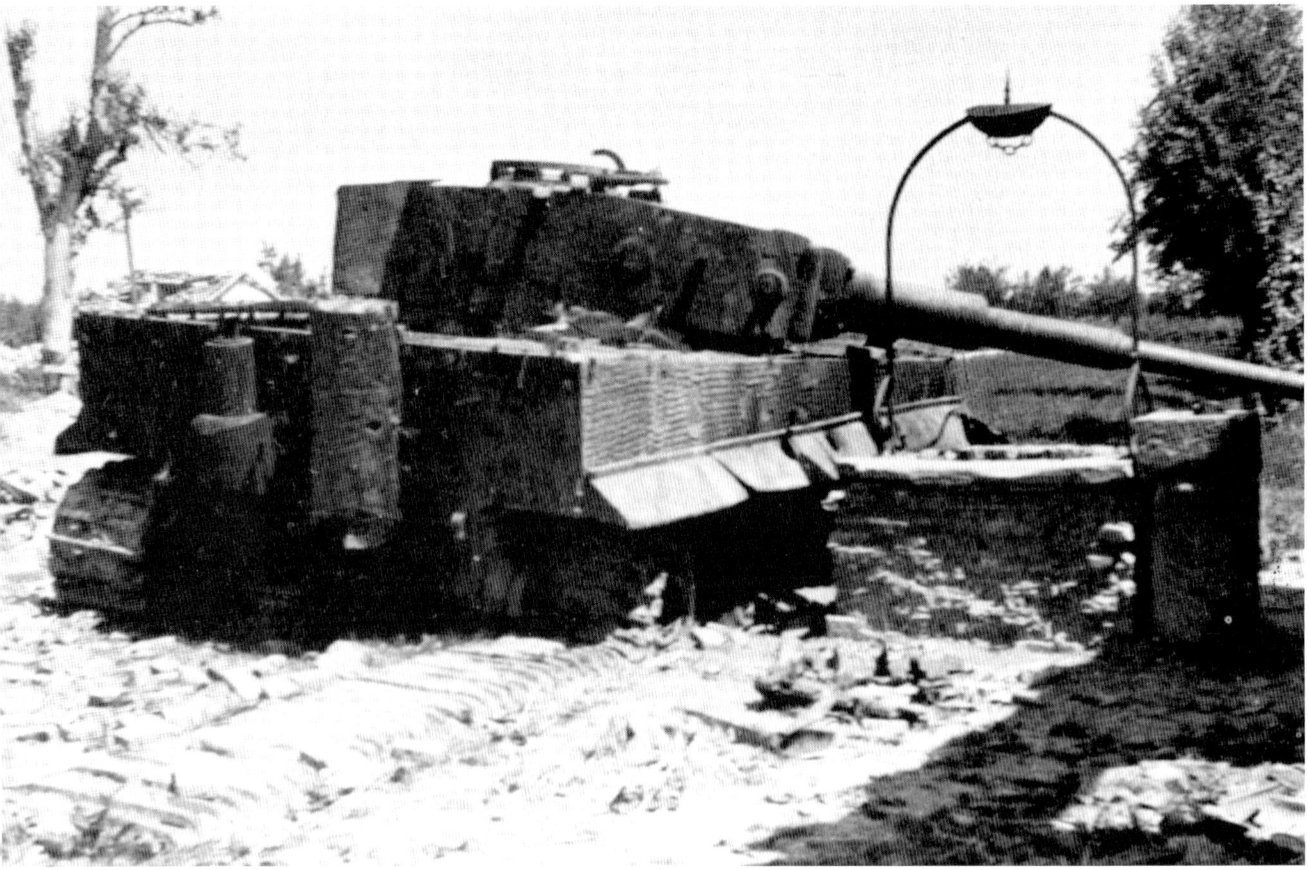

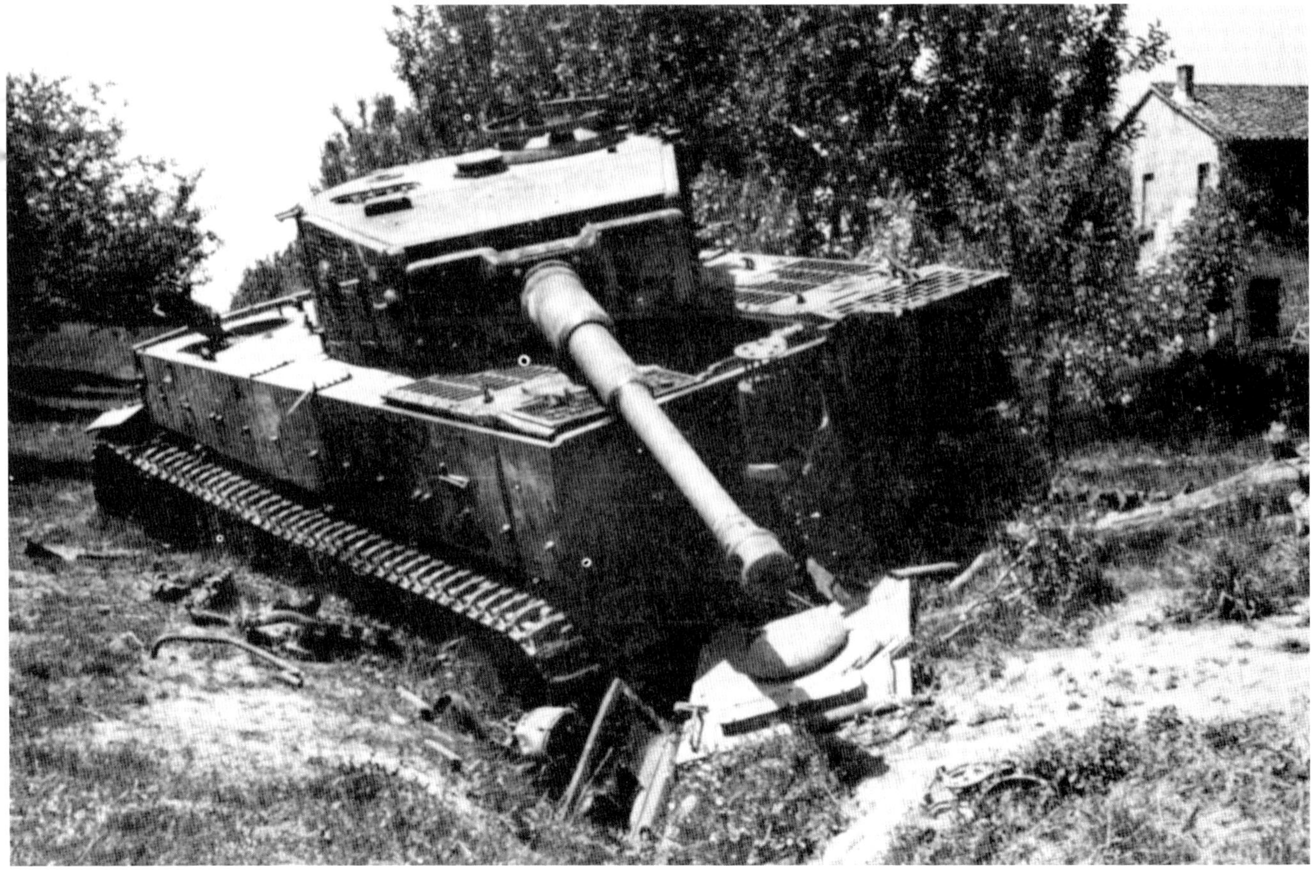

Chapter Two

Battles in Holland and Belgium

Following the Allies' successful advance through France in the summer of 1944, Holland and Belgium were now under threat. Plans were immediately drawn-up, predominantly led by British forces, for taking a series of nine bridges, the last bridge being in the city of Arnhem over the Rhine river. It was intended that airborne and land forces would liberate the Dutch cities of Eindhoven, Nijmegen and Arnhem and then advance into Germany, thus ending the war earlier than anticipated. However, unbeknown to the Allied planners, German forces recuperating in Holland were strong and determined. In particular there were two powerful Panzer divisions, 9th SS Panzer Division 'Hohenstaufen' and the 10th SS Panzer Division 'Frundsberg', resting well behind enemy lines. They had been sent to what was considered to be a relatively undisturbed area around Arnhem to rest and refit after being battered in Normandy. These were veteran soldiers, well armed, and supported by a good array of armour.

When the audacious Allied assault was finally launched on 17 September 1944, the US 82nd and 101st Airborne Divisions quickly consolidated their positions, taking the bridge town of Eindhoven and reaching Nijmegen, but they faltered against un-expected heavy German resistance. At Arnhem, the situation was much worse, with Allied troops finding themselves entangled in thick unrelenting fighting against tough, well-seasoned Waffen-SS Panzer troops. To exacerbate matters, there were other elite German forces in the area too, supporting the main Panzer divisions including SS-Unterführerschule kampfgruppen and some 400 troops from the 16th SS-Sturmbataillon, a number of Dutch SS police, Heer and Luftwaffe ground troops.

It did not take long before the Allies ran into difficulty. However, the Germans soon discovered how tough the British airborne troops were. What followed in Arnhem was a battle that degenerated into house-to-house and hand-to-hand fighting. Over the next few days heavy battles raged in and around Arnhem. Both sides became exhausted; the Germans were first to receive reinforcements. The Schwere Panzer Abteilung 506, which consisted of a number of Tiger tanks, were quickly moved in as a blocking unit to support units of the 'Frundsberg' division. The German armour was no match for the British and so remnants of the assault units were ordered to withdraw on the night of 25/26 September. Battered and depleted British forces then withdrew across the Lower Rhine at Oosterbeek and retreated south.

The battle of Arnhem had been a complete military failure for the Allies. Although the Germans had been severely weakened by months of fighting in France, they had inflicted a heavy blow on their foe in Holland.

For the next several weeks German forces on the Western Front continued to recoup and refit with additional armour and troops that were scraped up from the already depleted Eastern Front. For some time German planners were already gathering their troops for what was to be Germany's final attempt to regain the military initiative in the West. It would be a bold offensive in Belgium, code named *Wacht am Rhein* (Watch on the Rhine).

Here in the Ardennes a substantial number of divisions had been assigned to the area, including four crack Waffen-SS divisions: 1st SS 'Leibstandarte Adolf Hitler', 2nd SS 'Das Reich', 9th SS 'Hohenstaufen', and 12th SS 'Hitlerjugend'. The equipment used by both the Wehrmacht and SS armoured formations in the Ardennes was generally good, although by this late period of the war it was in short supply. The forces committed to the battle zone contained a number of independent self-propelled anti-tank and heavy tank battalions and several assault gun brigades, which were battalion size formations. There were four Schwere Panzerjäger battalions, nominally equipped with a mix of Jagdpanthers, Panzerjäger IVs, and Sturmgeschütz IIIs. The Schwere Panzer battalions contained the famous Tiger heavy tanks. Three of these units were committed in the Ardennes and the 501st SS was attached to the Leibstandarte. The lead element of the 501st SS Schwere Panzer Abteilung was commanded by the veteran armoured ace Obersturmbannführer Joachim Peiper, commander of the 1st SS Panzer-Regiment.

The German forces in the Ardennes comprised of the 6th Panzer Army which contained all the four SS Panzer divisions and was given the task to tear holes in the American lines between the Losheim Gap and Monschau. To the south of the 6th Army's sector lay General der Panzertruppen Hasso von Manteuffel's 5th Panzer Army and General Erich Brandenberger's 7th Army, which was the southernmost of the three armies committed to the offensive. Altogether the five Panzer and Panzer-grenadier divisions and thirteen infantry-type divisions, consisting of Fallschirmjäger and Volksgrenadier troops, were to be unleashed through the Belgium and Luxembourg countryside.

The offensive began in the early morning of 16 December 1944 along the German front from Monschau in the north to Echternach on the Luxembourg border. In the north the 6th Panzer Army inflicted the heaviest barrage of fire. At least 657 guns and howitzers of various calibre and 340 Nebelwerfers were directed on American positions between Hofen and the Losheim Gap. Once the barrage of fire subsided, the Volksgrenadiers, many going into battle for the first time, crashed into action closely followed by the tanks and elite Waffen-SS Panzer divisions. The spearhead of the 6th Panzer Army was formed by I SS Panzer-Korps, which had been tasked with smashing through American lines between Hollerath and Krewinkel and driving through to Liege-Huy sector. Within the first twenty-four hours of the offensive SS tanks continued to exploit the American defences using every means at its disposal to annihilate all enemy resistance. Yet, in spite of the successful German advance through the Ardennes, the Allies soon began to recover from the initial surprise, and resistance stiffened day by day. By 22 December the Americans began stemming the German drive. Coupled with the lack of fuel and the constant congestions on the narrow roads, many German units were brought to a standstill. The fuel shortages were so bad that on 23 December Peiper's Kampfgruppe destroyed their vehicles, and his remaining 1,000 men set out on foot for the German lines. The remnants of the Kampfgruppe then linked up with the 'Leibstandarte' just before dawn on Christmas day.

Along the entire Ardennes front German soldiers were becoming increasingly exhausted. For days and nights, in the wet and cold, they had pushed westwards towards a promised victory. Nourished by their early success and apparent lack of resistance, their forces began to wither as shortages of rations, lack of sleep, and the constant shelling and bombing from aerial attacks drained their energy. With the armoured spearheads ruptured by broken lines of communication and lack of fuel, the Ardennes offensive began to ground to a halt less than two weeks after it had begun.

In a drastic attempt to assist the failing drive to the Meuse River, additional troops were thrown in to launch a new offensive in Alsace, where the Americans had drained their forces in order to send reinforcements north into the Ardennes. The code-name was 'Nordwind', and it was launched in earnest on New Year's Day with eight divisions spearheaded by an SS Korps consisting of the 17th SS Panzergrenadier-Division 'Götz von Berlichingen' and the 36th Volksgrenadier-Division. At first the offensive went relatively well, but heavy resistances soon forced the Germans back. The subsequent commitment of the 10th SS Panzer-Division 'Frundsberg' and the 6th SS Gebirgs-Division 'Nord' failed to alter the situation in the area.

During the first days of January 1945, the weather became even more difficult, with temperatures falling to around zero. Fighting through fog, sleet and deep snow caused discouragement and pessimism to spread on both sides. Around the strategic town of Bastogne the Germans were eventually forced on the offensive and driven back. Nearly 12,000 German troops were killed attempting to capture Bastogne and 900 Americans died defending it, with another 3,000 killed outside the perimeter.

From the pulverising effects of ground and aerial attacks, the Germans left behind 450 tanks and armoured vehicles.

The defeat outside Bastogne was yet another major blow to the German command and marked the turning point of the offensive. All across their battered front fighting had begun to get harder and resistance was even more difficult to overcome. Troops constantly found themselves beating the enemy at terrible cost only to find, a few miles on, fresh, well-armed American troops waiting for them.

With so many Allied troops being employed in the Ardennes, it slowly forced Hitler to realize how dangerous the war in the West had become. On 8 January, with more than 100,000 Germans dead on the battlefield, the Führer grudgingly ordered the remnants of the forward units to fall back to a line running south from Dochamps, in the Samree-Baraque de Fraiture area, to Longchamps, 5 miles north of Bastogne. Even more significant were orders for the mighty elite SS Panzer divisions to go over to the defensive. Days later these units were withdrawn from the front altogether. The remaining Fallschirmjäger and regular forces left defending the Ardennes sector were then withdrawn and all other units were back over the Rhine by 10 February, preparing to defend German soil for the first time.

Two well camouflaged PanzerKampfwagen V Ausf.G Panthers advance through a French village in August 1944. On the Western Front, Allied airpower was dominant and severely hindered movement of the German Panzer units, making camouflage on all vehicles a priority.

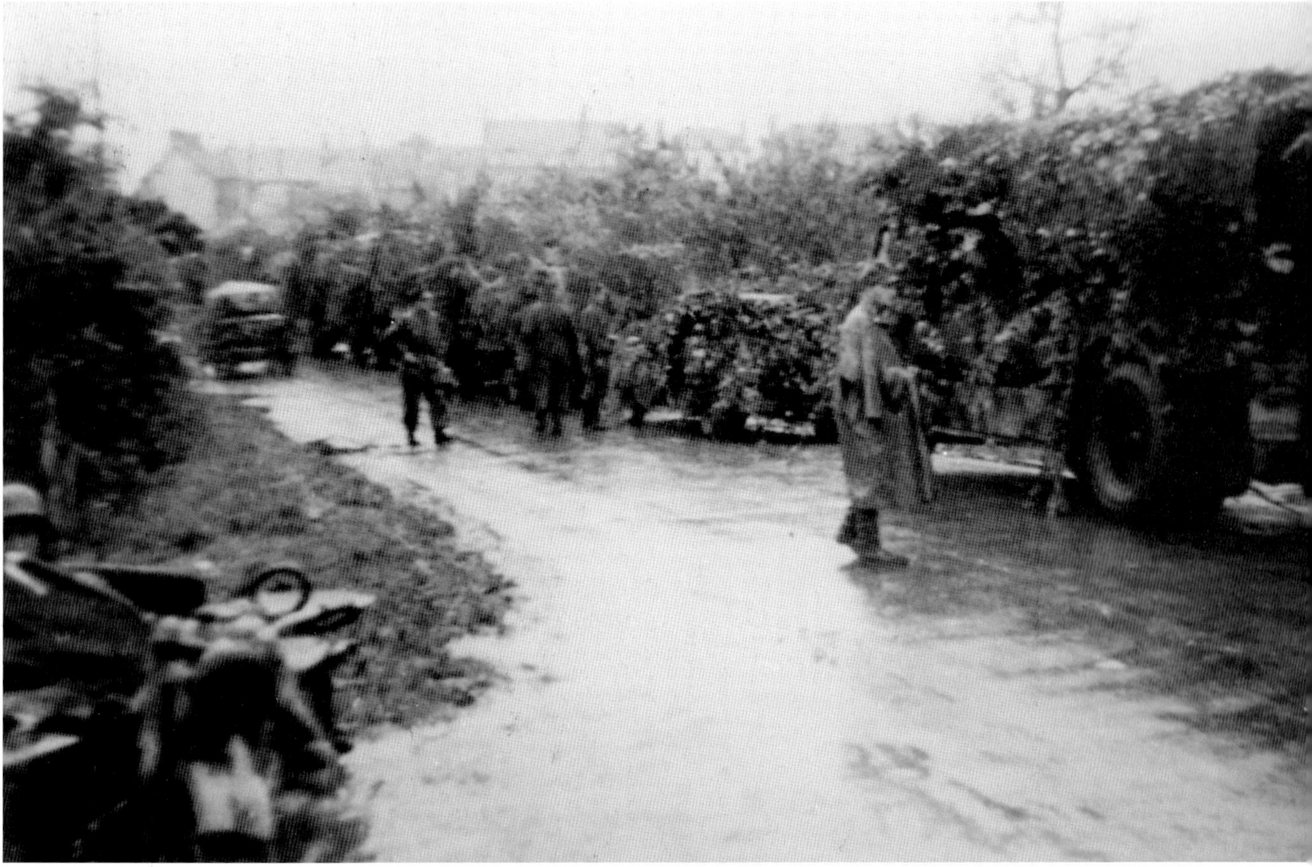

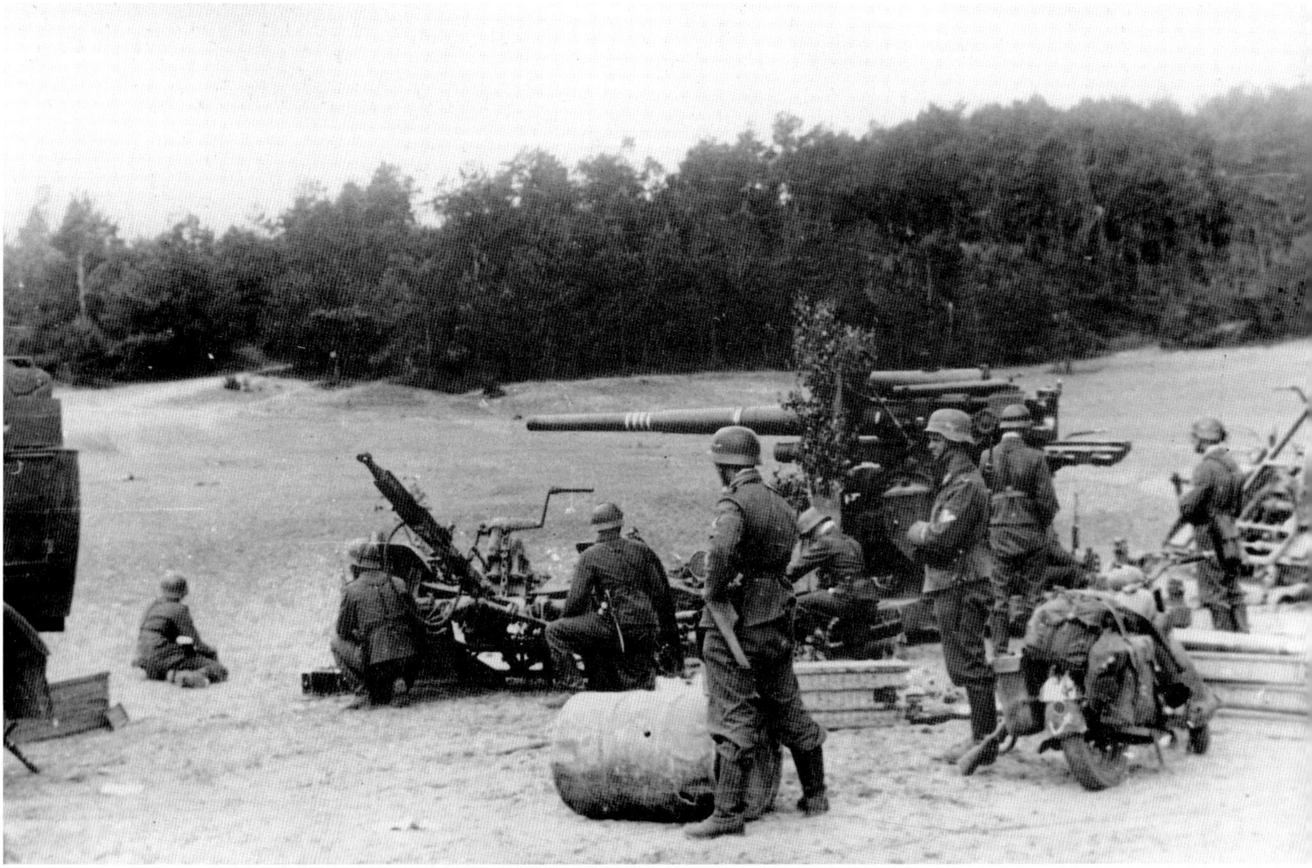

(**Opposite, above**) A column of well camouflaged vehicles stationary along a road in Holland in September 1944. Many German armoured units had been decimated in France from the constant Allied aerial attacks and those that were fortunate enough to escape the slaughter withdrew north of the Seine and into Belgium and Holland.

(**Opposite, below**) A Luftwaffe 8.8cm FlaK crew in a field. The weapon has been directed in a horizontal position against possible ground targets. Note the four kill rings painted on the gun tube.

(**Above, left**) A Panther advances along a road in September 1944. By this period losses in Panthers had reached unprecedented levels.

(**Above, right**) Fallschirmjäger troops on the move inside a camouflaged Kubelwagen advance along a narrow road in Holland in September 1944. Fighting in Normandy for the Fallschirmjäger division had been severe and only a few units managed to escape from the Falaise Pocket. All that was left of the division formed into what was known as a Kampfgruppe and retreated towards the German Eifel area. In September 1944 the Fallschirmjäger Kampfgruppe participated in a short battle for the Wallendorf bridgehead supported by elements of the Polizei Battalion and the 2nd Panzer and Panzer Lehr division, where units drove back US forces back over the Our river in Luxembourg.

A later Panther Ausf.G advances through a badly damaged town. The tank is painted in a factory-applied camouflage scheme. This Panzer belongs to Panzer-Regiment's I Abteilung, 3 Kompanie, and is the second vehicle of the second platoon.

Two photographs showing Fallschrimjäger and grenadiers smiling for the camera as they march along a road in Holland using wheelbarrows to transport their weapons, ammunitions and personal equipment. By this period of the war, vehicle movement during daylight hours was kept to a minimum due to Allied air attacks, compelling many units to march on foot to their selective positions.

Civilians pass a knocked out Lorraine-based Marder I. The Marder I fulfilled its mission of quickly providing mobile anti-tank fire to the infantry and Panzer regiments. However, in France, where this vehicle mainly operated, during the bitter fighting that raged in the Normandy sector, many of these vehicles were lost as troops withdrew to the German frontier. By February/March 1945 only six of the Marder Is were operating in the entire German Army.

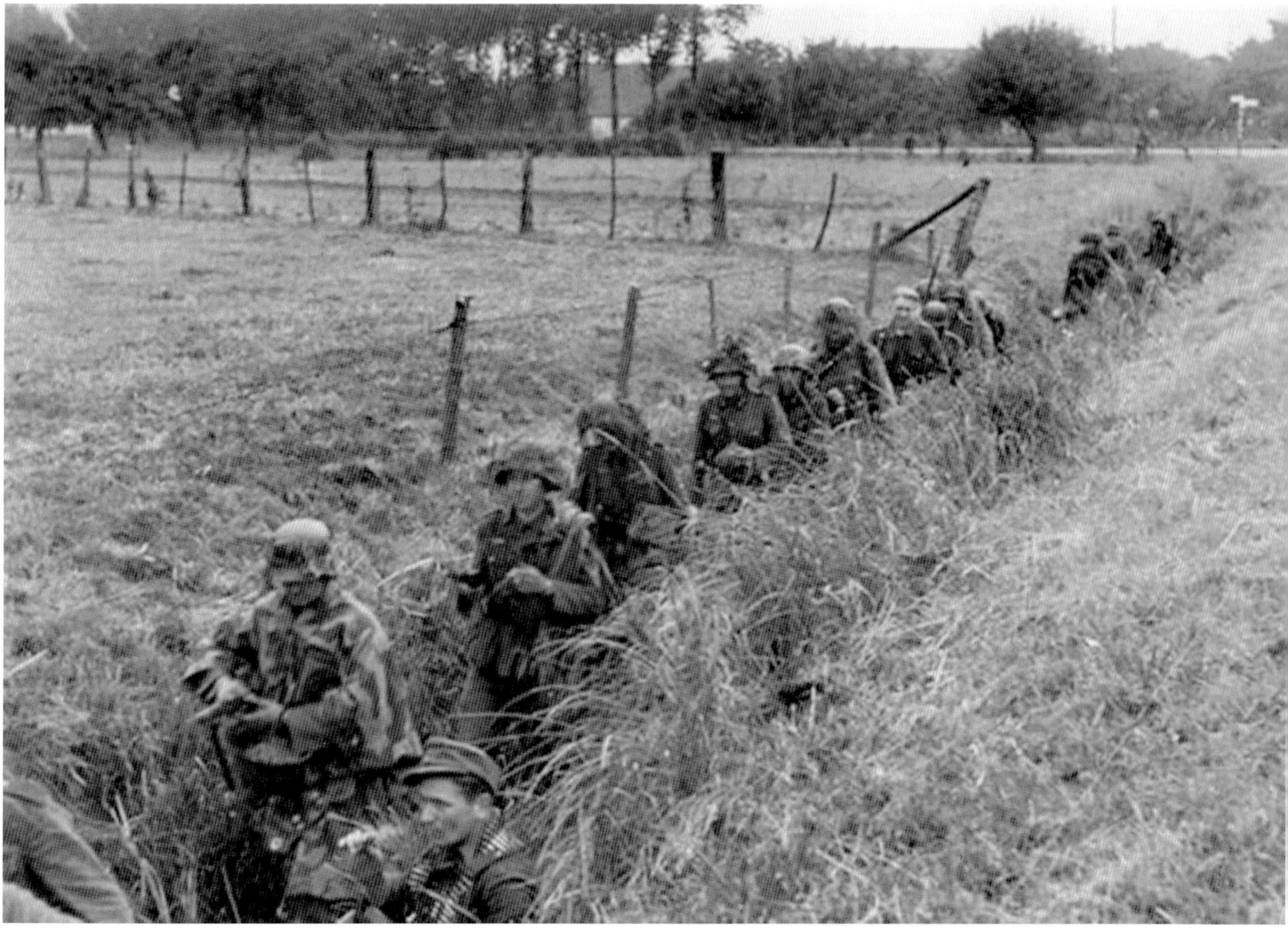

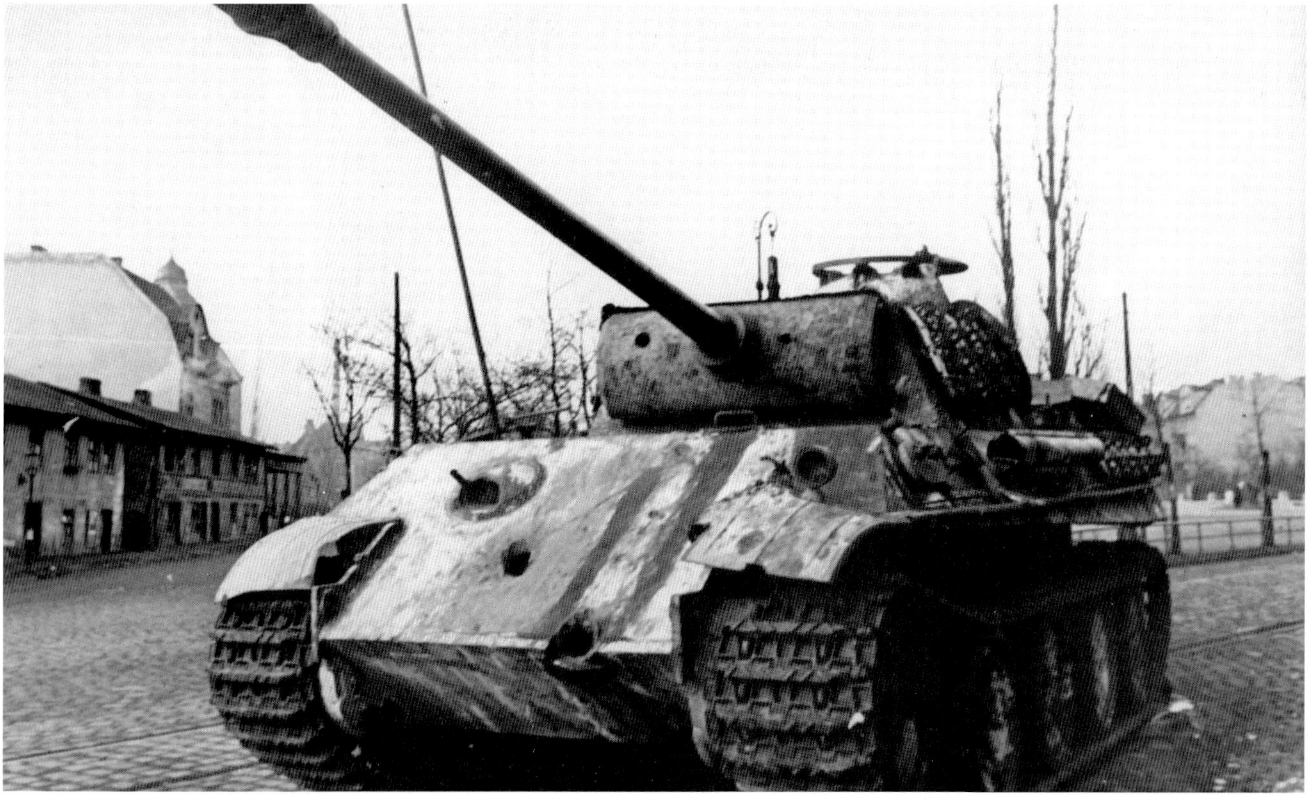

(**Opposite, above**) In a trench grenadiers are seen on a march. Note the soldier nearest to the photographer who has a MG42 machine gun belt around his neck.

(**Above**) An interesting photograph showing troops armed with the deadly Panzerfaust and stove pipe in a French town in the summer of 1944.

(**Opposite, below**) A knocked out Panther. Many of these Panthers were sent to the western front to stop to stop the allied advance. However, many of them stumbled into ambushes against well seasoned US tank crews.

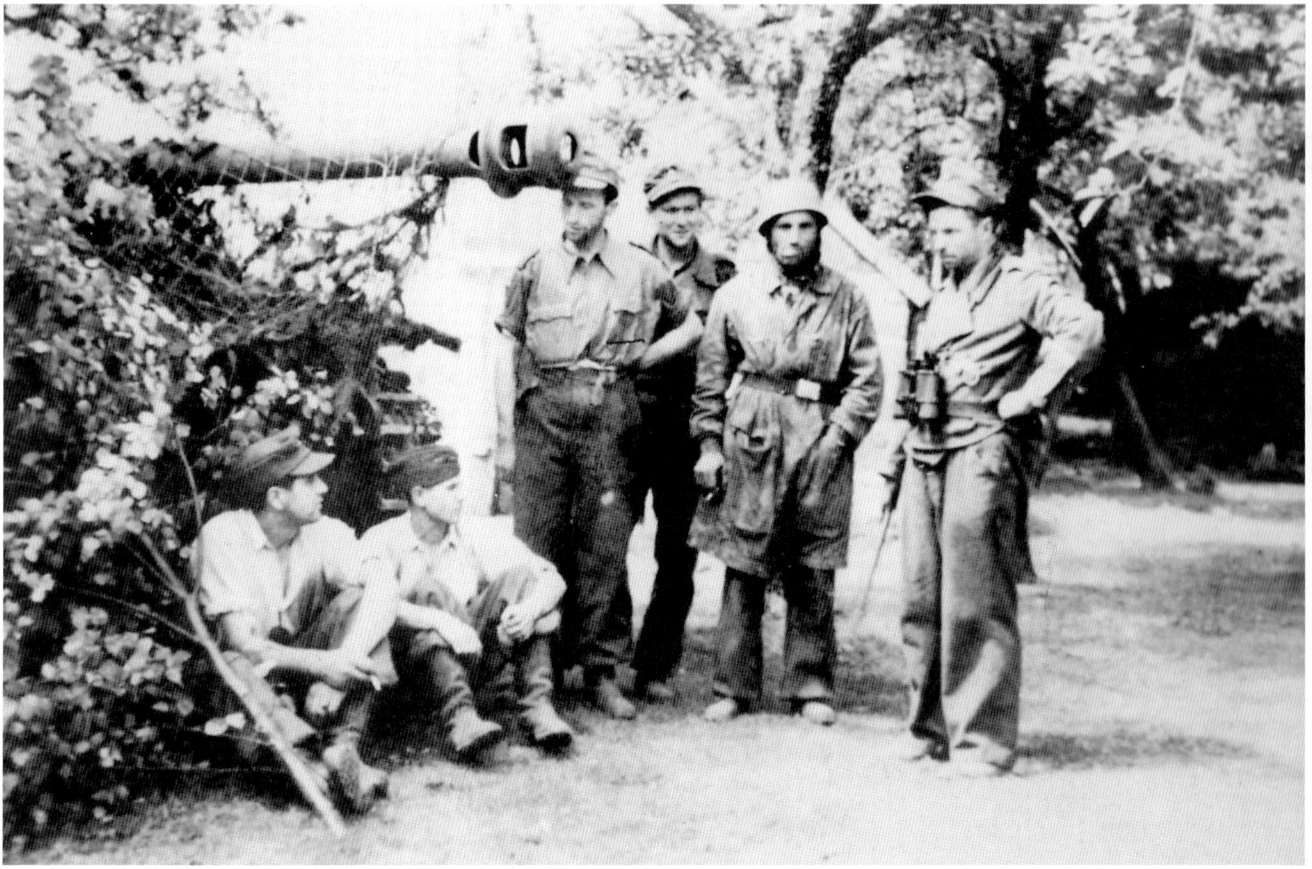

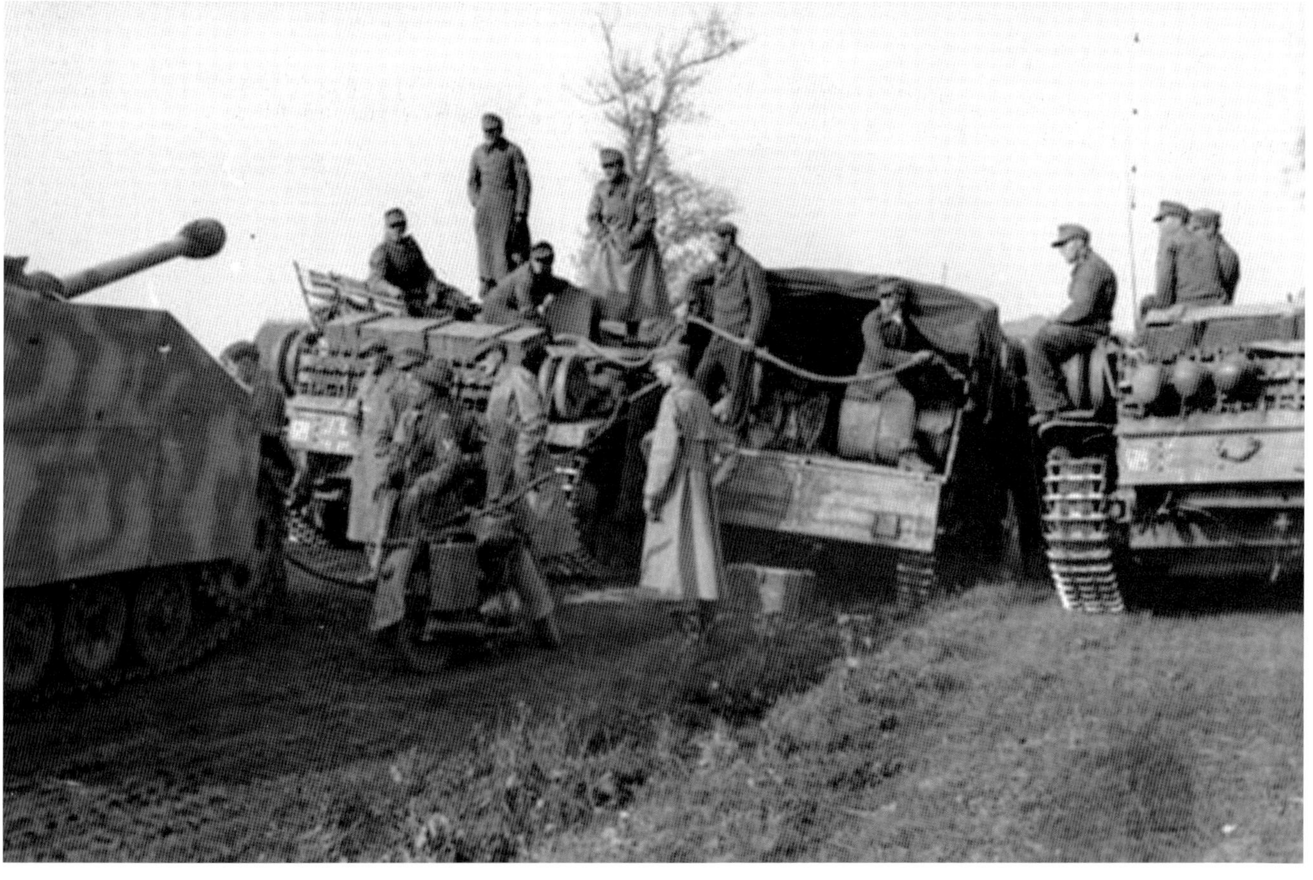

(**Opposite, above**) A group of Luftwaffe ground truppen pose for the camera next to a StuG.III Ausf.G. The soldiers wear a variety of uniforms including Fallschirmjäger, assault gun crewman's field grey uniforms, jump smocks and tropical uniforms.

(**Opposite, below**) A group of StuG.III Ausf.Gs are being refueled from a Maultier cargo truck. By late 1944 fuel was a rare commodity for both assault and Panzer crews. Some vehicles on the Western Front were abandoned due to the lack of fuel.

(**Above**) A Panzer crew rest in a clearing with a member of the Fallschirmjäger Truppen. The Pz.Kpfw IV is well camouflaged with sapplings in order to conceal it from both ground and aerial recognition.

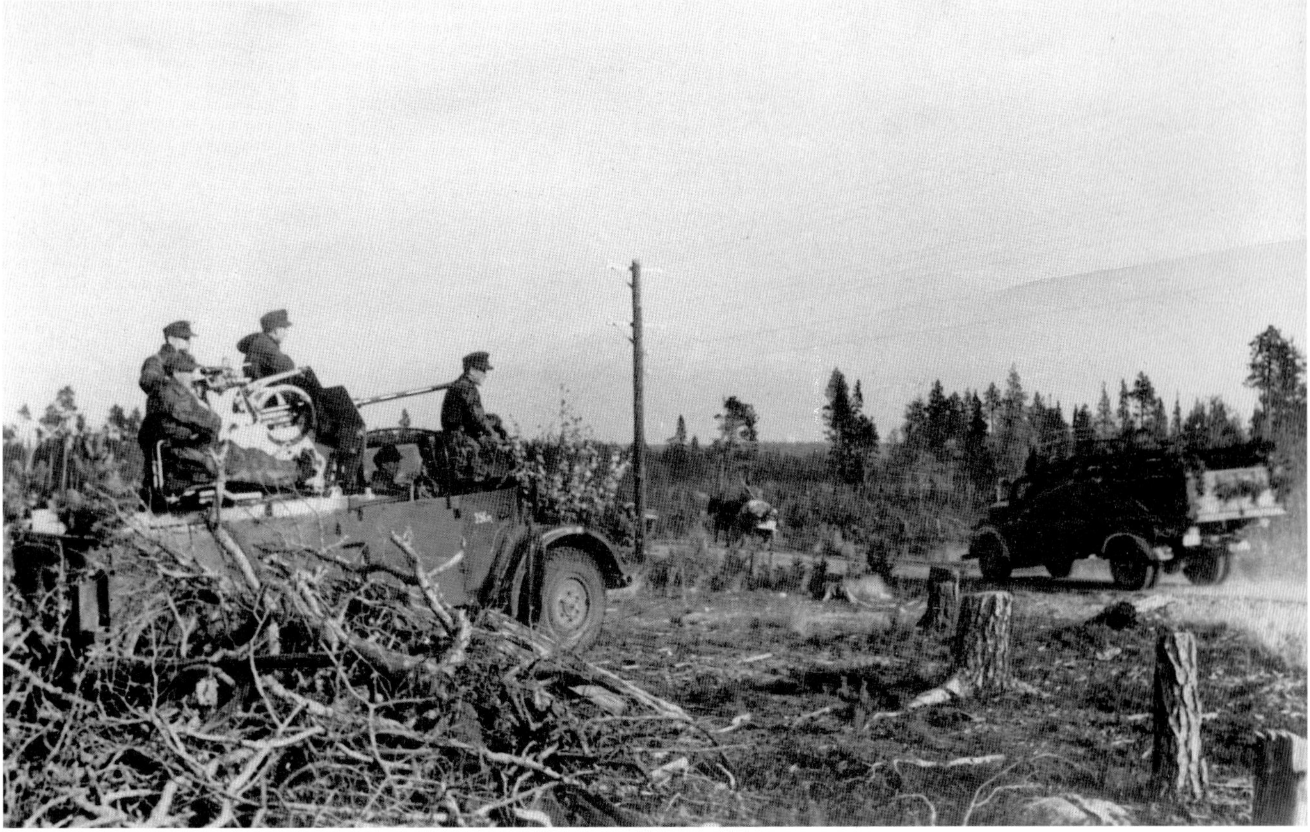

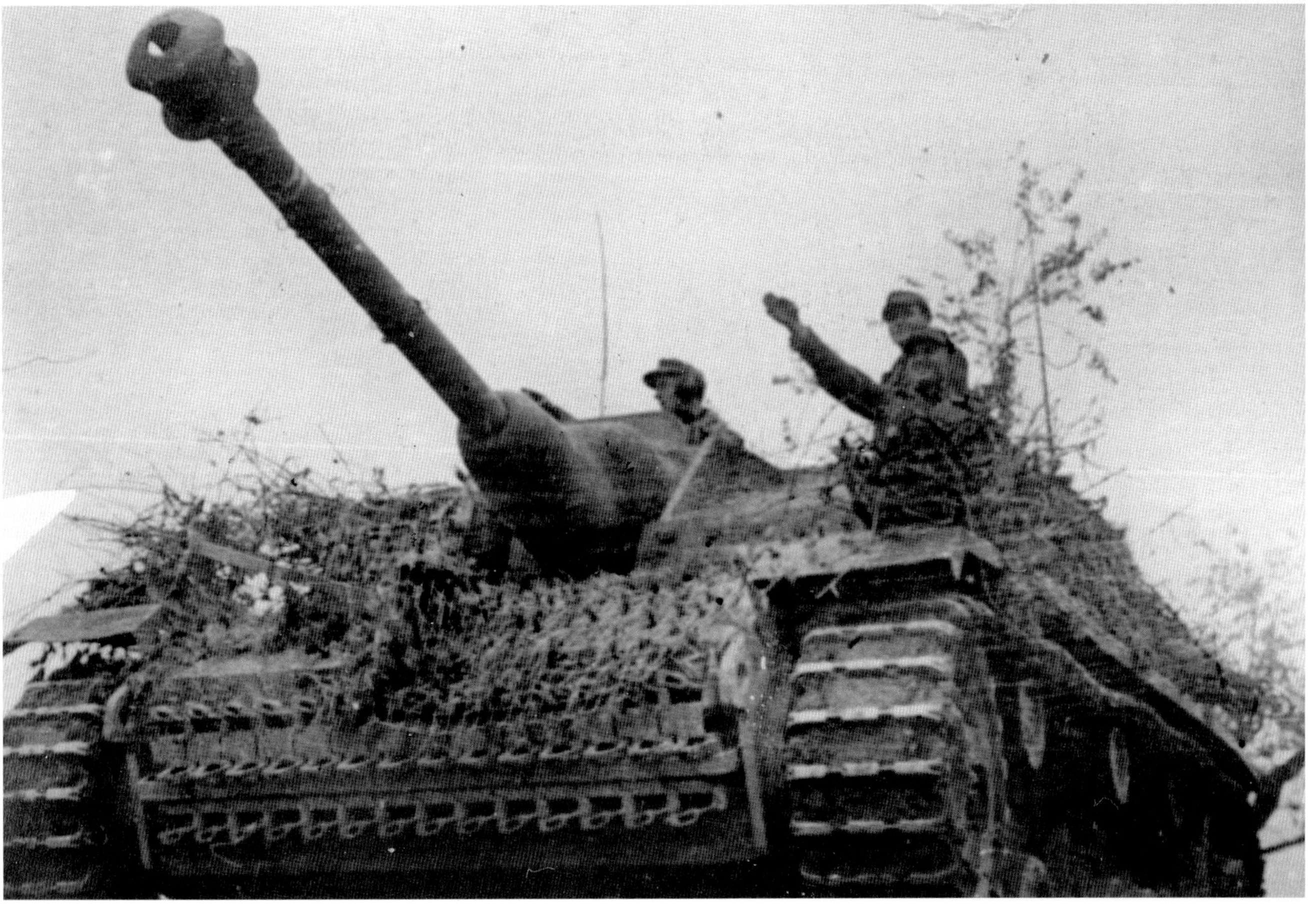

(**Opposite, above**) A FlaK gun has been mounted on a wheeled vehicle in Belgium. In front of the FlaK crew a supply truck carrying troops to the front can be seen.

(**Opposite, below**) A StuG.III Ausf.G can be seen on the move. A crew member waves to the photographer. This assault gun is armed with the punchy 7.7cm StuK 40 L/48 gun which is housed in a cast Topfblende (pot mantle). Note the two kill rings painted around the gun tube, near the double-baffle muzzle brake.

(**Above**) During the early phase of operations in the Ardennes in December 1944 showing commanding officers inside a Volkswagen Type 166 Schwimmwagen, which literally meant floating/swimming car. This amphibious four-wheel drive off-roader was used extensively by both the Wehrmacht and Waffen-SS on the Western Front. The Type 166 was the most numerous mass-produced amphibious car in history.

A stationary Sd.Kfz.251 halftrack with some of the crew members conversing. A washing line has been erected between two trees and the crews underwear can be seen hung across the line to dry. Note the M35 steel helmets attached to the vehicle's side armour in order to give it better armoured protection. The Sd.Kfz.251 was used extensively during the latter half of the war to transport Panzergrenadiers to the forward edge of the battlefield. Despite being in the main lightly armoured, they could maintain a relatively modest speed and manoeuvre across country and keep up with the fast-moving spearheads.

(**Opposite, above**) An Sd.Kfz.250 can be seen in a field as Panzergrenadiers pass on their way to the battlefront. The soldiers are wearing various combinations of the Wehrmacht reversible, padded two-piece winter suit.

(**Opposite, below**) Various armoured vehicles including two Panzerkampfwagen IVs and halftracks supporting an advance through a wooded area in Belgium. Using a number of halftracks was the most effective and quickest way of being transported either to the battlefield, or being withdrawn to another line of defence. When the halftracks arrived at the edge of a battlefield, the troops were able to quickly dismount to take up positions.

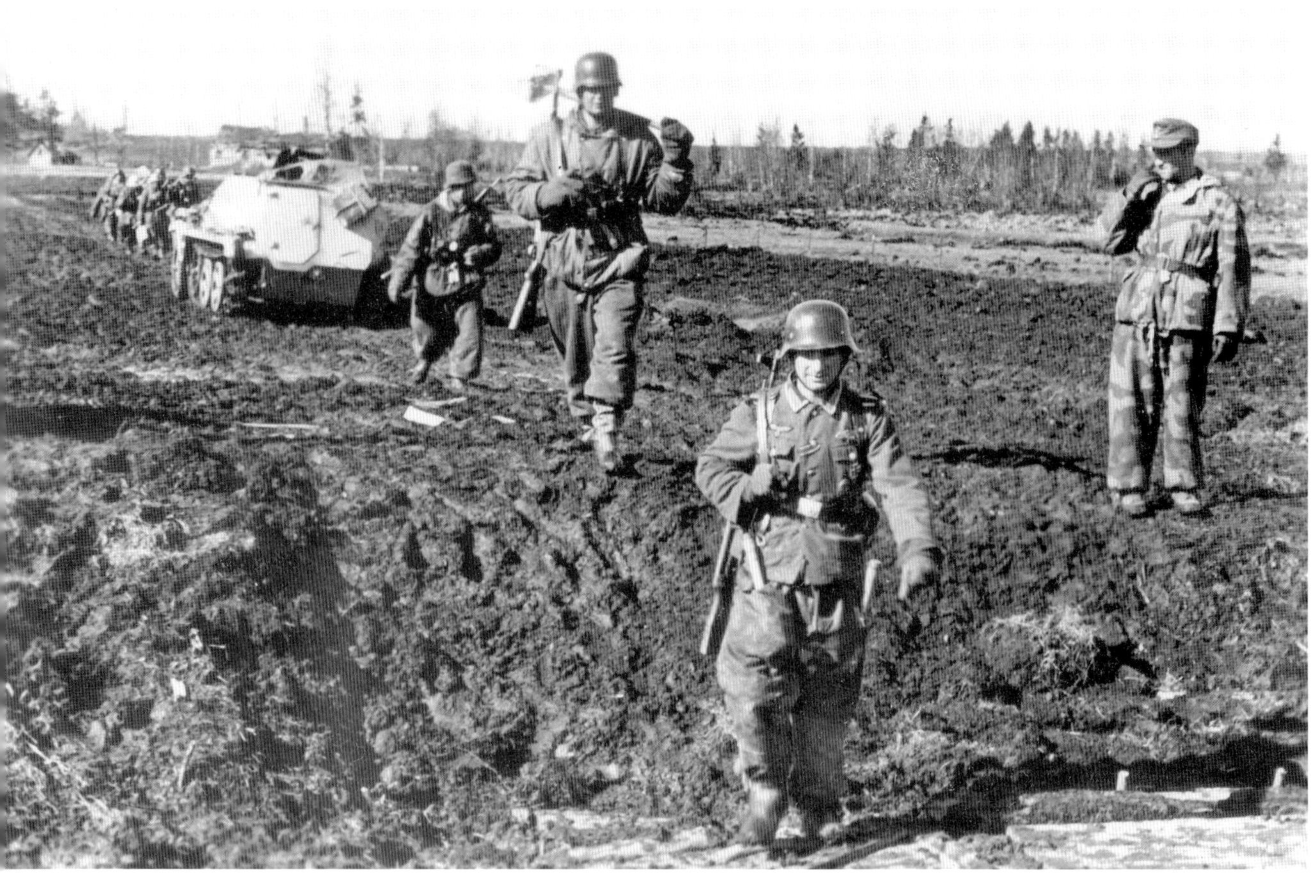

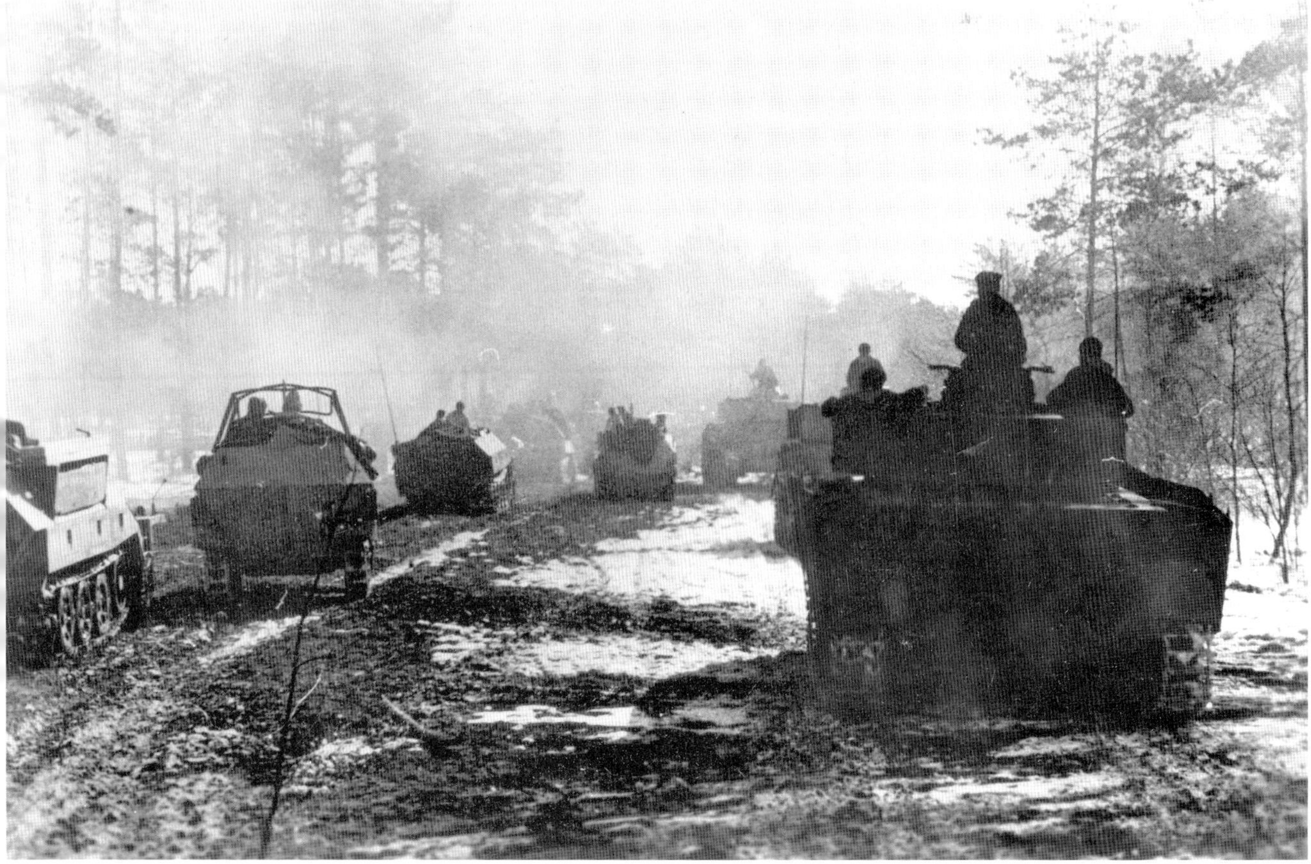

(**Above**) Two Sd.Kfz.251, one an Ausf.C and the other an Ausf.D, pull alongside each other. The crew appear to be exchanging details. The Ausf.C mounts the typical frame antenna; the Ausf.D has no antenna. Both mount the MG34 machine gun with splinter shield.

(**Opposite, above**) Here a crewman prepares to launch his Panzerwerfer. He is standing on the open hatches, through which rockets are being passed. The back blast from the Nebelwerfer was very powerful and could often move a vehicle as large as this by a foot.

(**Opposite, below**) A Panzer crew converse with a commanding officer in thick snow during operations in Belgium in December 1944. By the end of December 1944 the whole position in the Ardennes was on the point of disintegration for the Germans. Action in Belgium had been a gruelling battle of attrition for both German and Allied units.

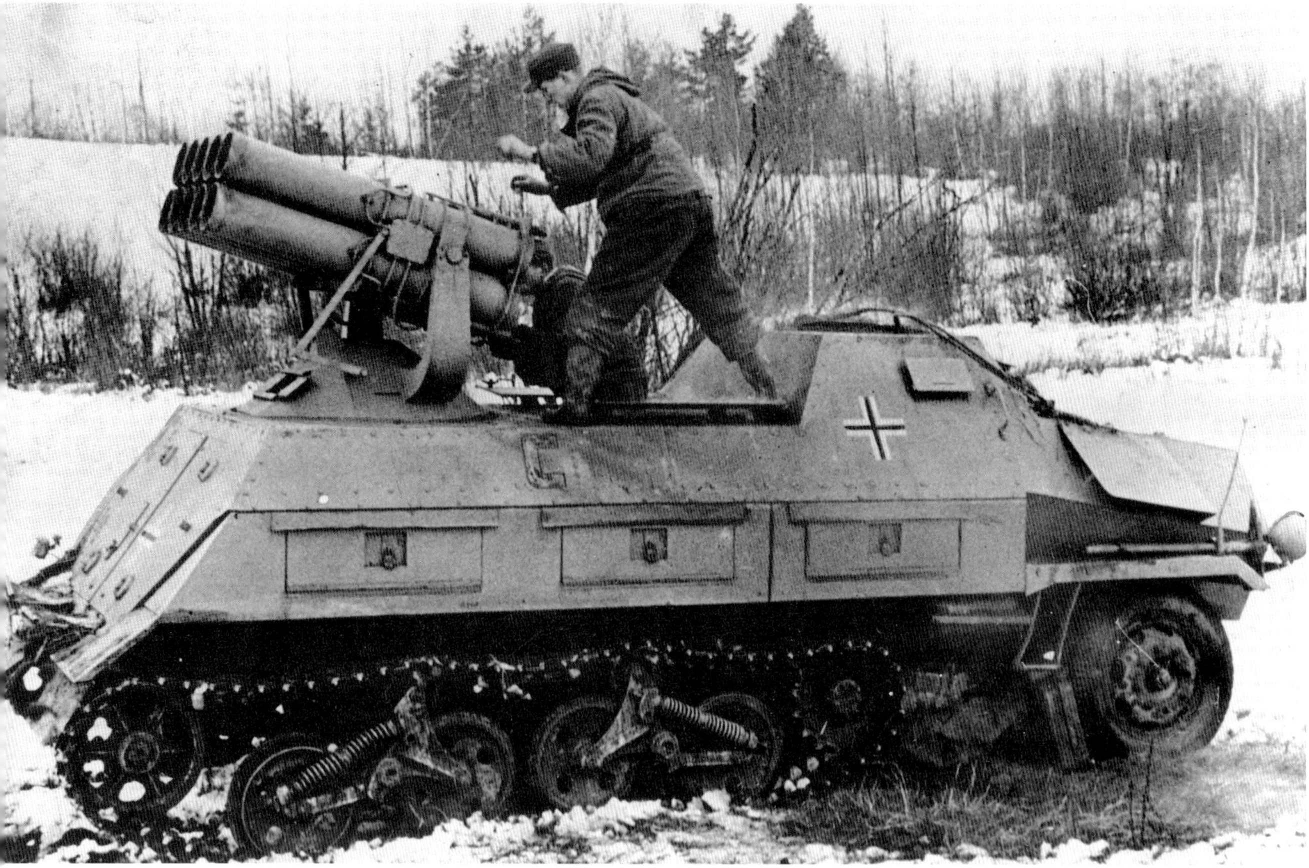

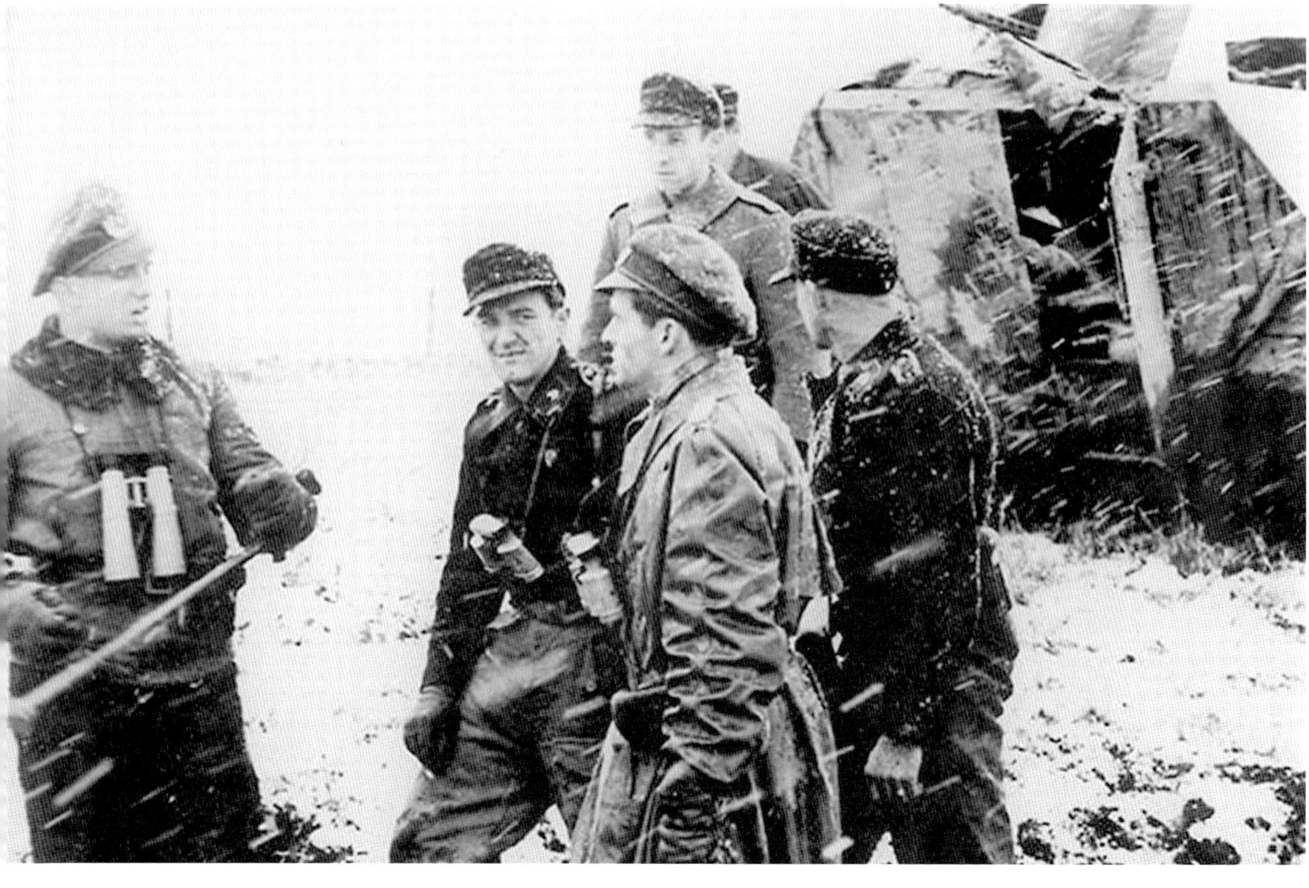

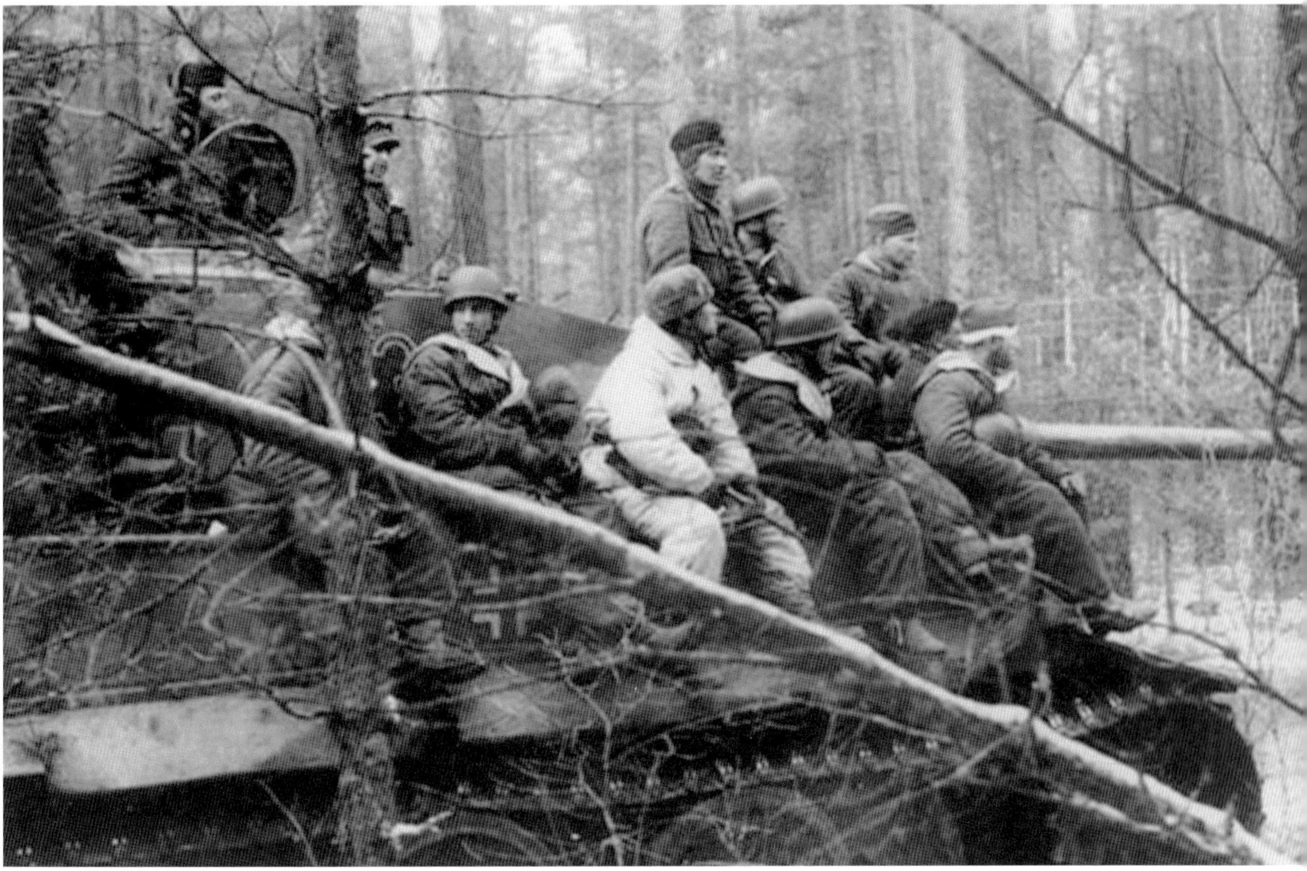

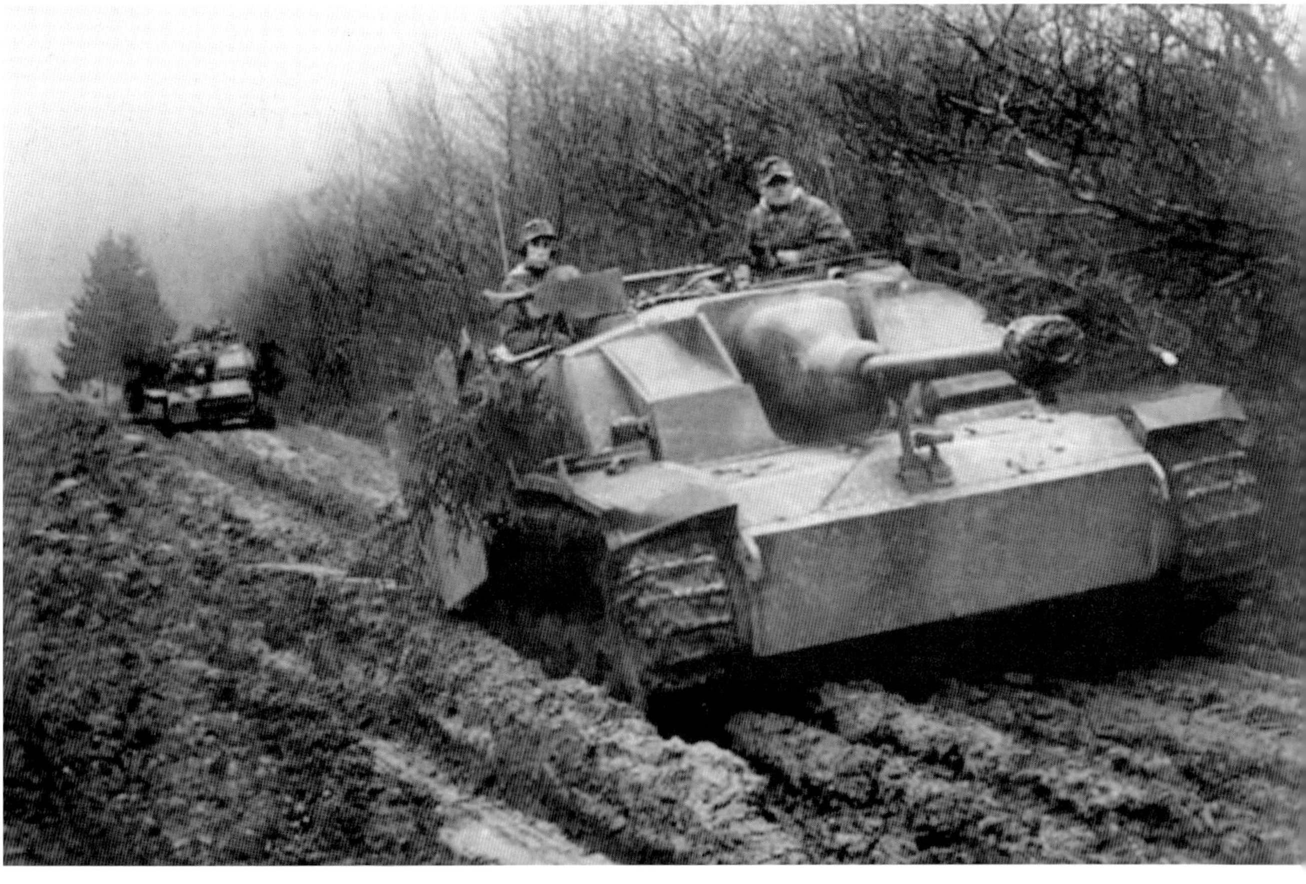

(**Opposite, above**) Fallschirmjäger truppen hitch a lift onboard a Tiger tank as German forces withdraw through a forest. By this time production of the Tiger I had been terminated in favour of the superior Tiger II or 'King Tiger'. However, numbers of the new machines were simply not enough to avert the catastrophe unfolding on both the Western and Eastern Fronts.

(**Opposite, below**) A StuG.IV churns along a muddy road in the Ardennes. This late production assault gun comprised a single 80mm-thick armour plate on the starboard side casemate front. Attached to the roof is a 360-degree mounted traverse MG42 for close defence. Note half of the vehicle's side skirt or Schürzen is missing and saplings can be seen attached to parts of the side armour.

(**Above**) In the Ardennes a Panzerkampfwagen IV has been concealed by the crew with wooden planks, foliage and branches from the surrounding trees. The Panzer is further concealed, parked next to a derelict building.

Obviously working in very cold conditions, the loader rams home a complete projectile in the FlaK 8.8cm gun. Note the shield forward of the pneumatic recuperator; the small cylinder on top of it is a cover for the mount for the indirect-fire RB1f sight, which was used when the gun was deployed in a conventional field artillery role.

(**Opposite, above**) A King Tiger rolls along a road followed by two motorcyclists armed with the MP40 machine gun pistols slung around their back for ease of carriage. Moving in the opposite direction is a column of American troops captured during the initial stages of the Ardennes offensive.

(**Opposite, below**) In the Ardennes a Waffen-SS StuG.IV moves across an open field passing captured American vehicles. Typical for this type, the assault gun mounts its StuK40 inside a cast pot mantlet or Topfblende. Note the extensive use of zimmerit anti-magnetic mine paste applied over the armoured plates of the vehicle. The near side track guard appears to have been damaged and is buckled upwards.

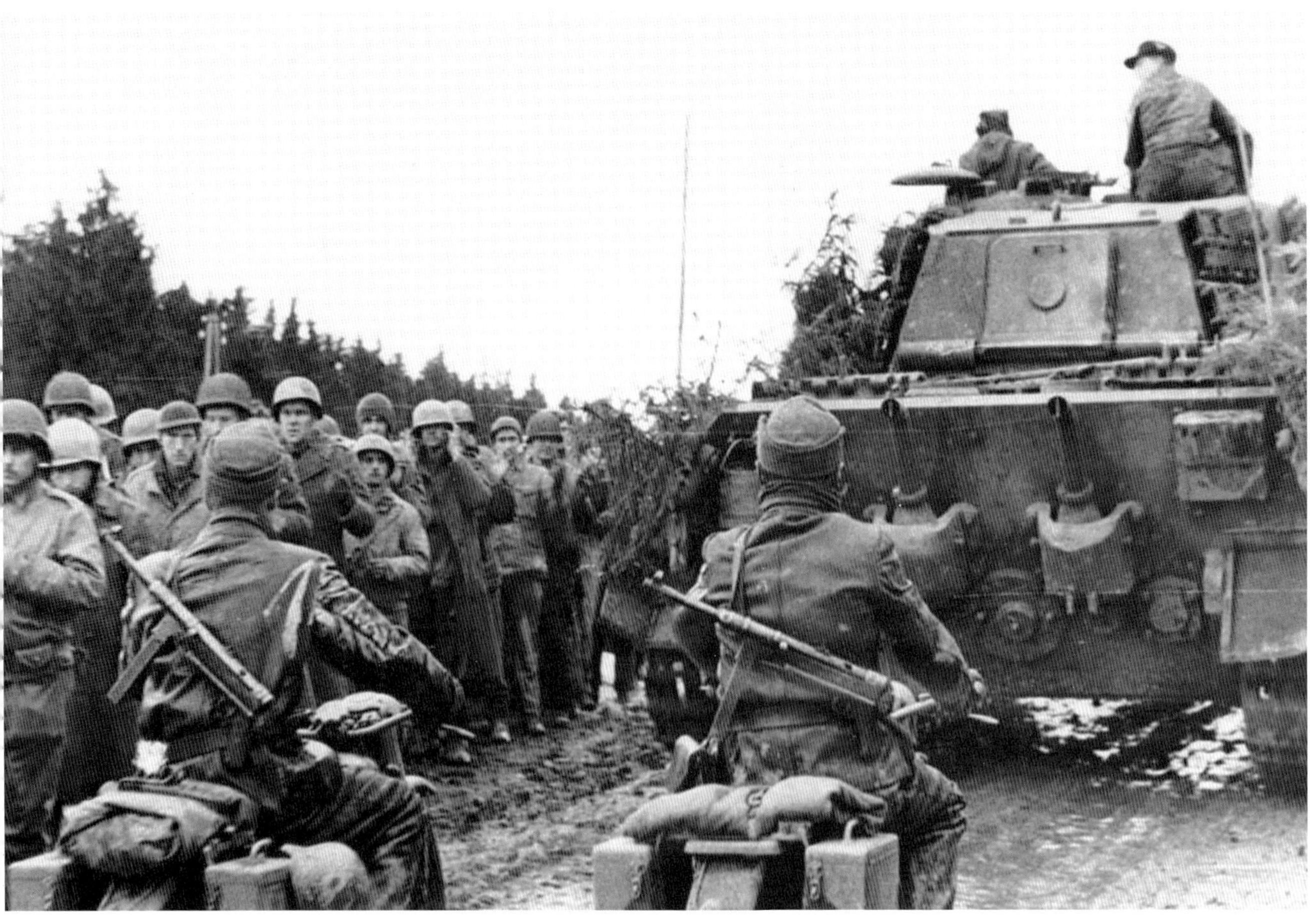

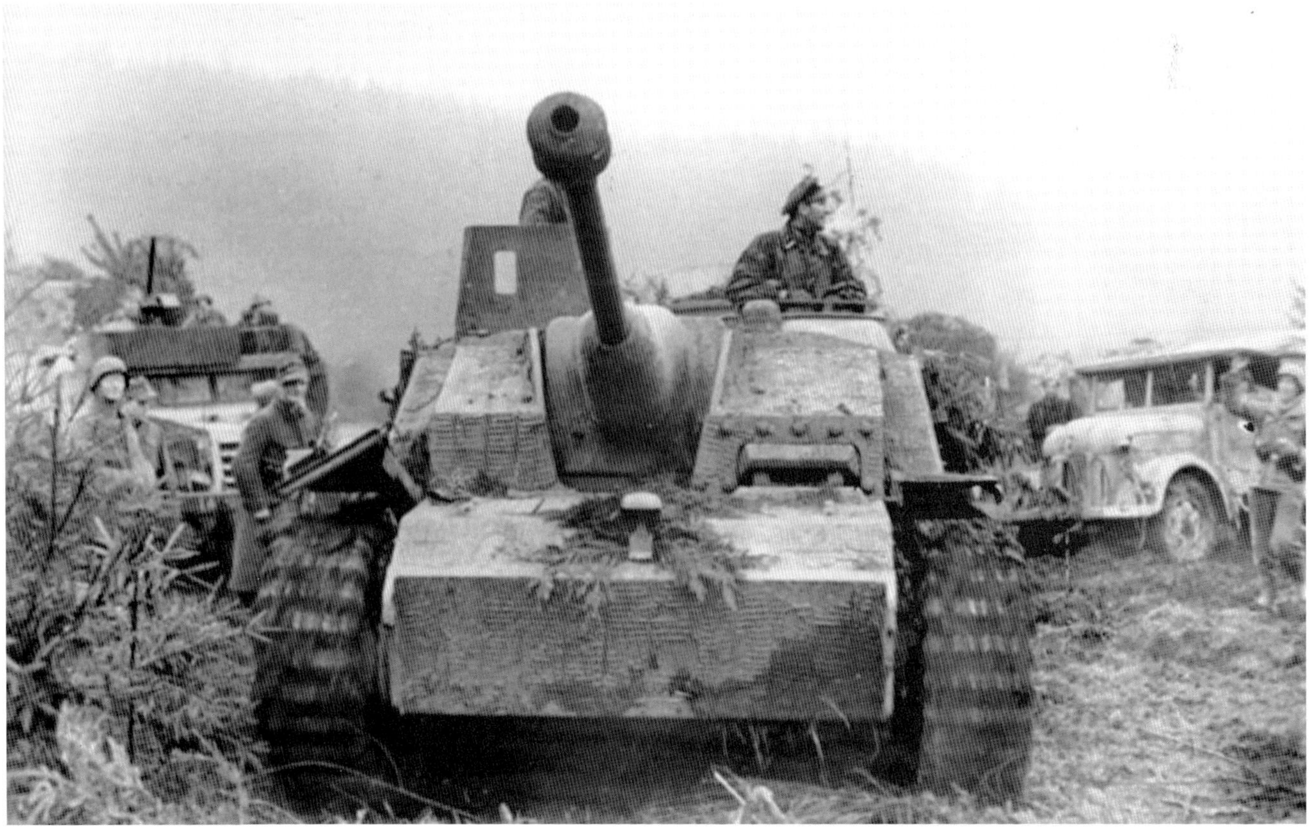

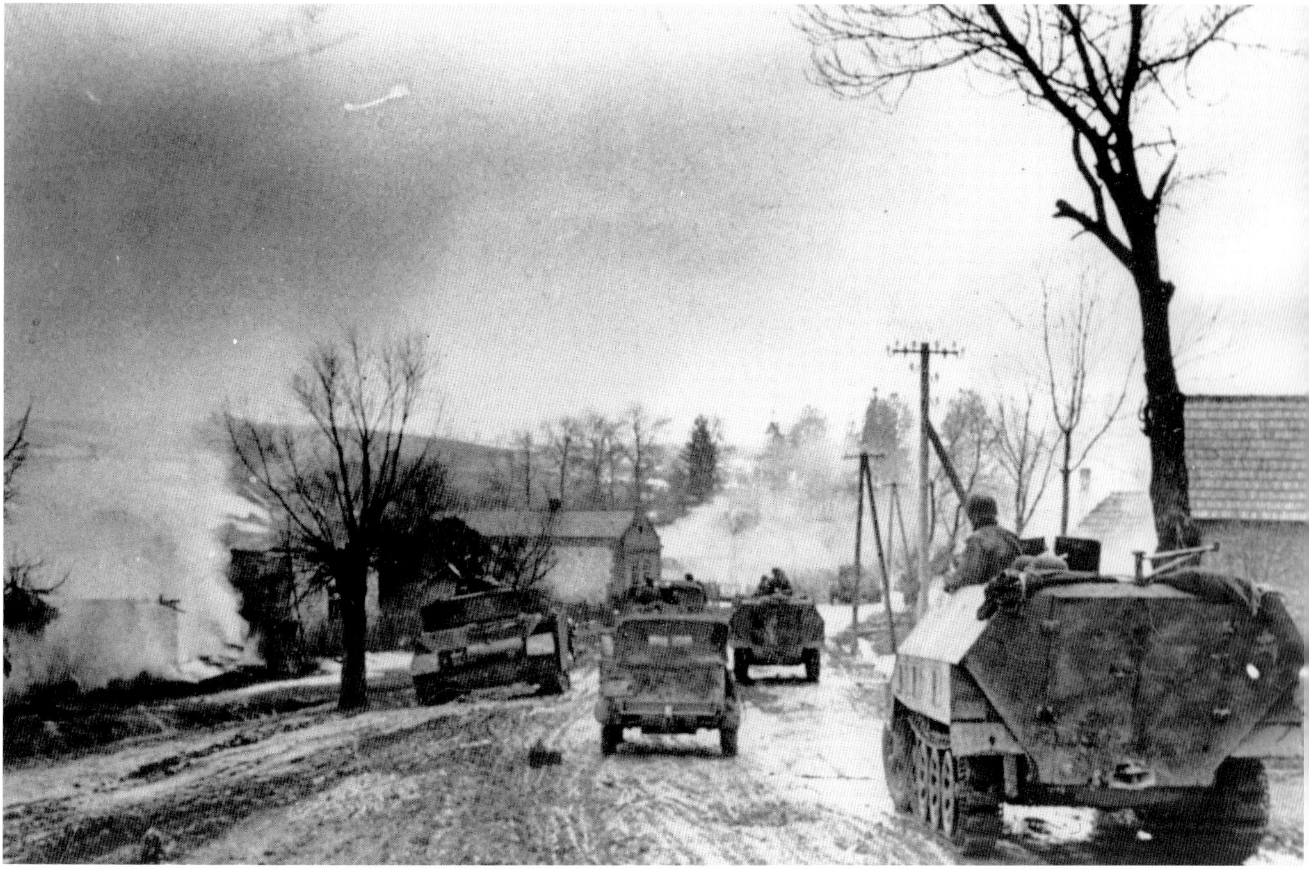

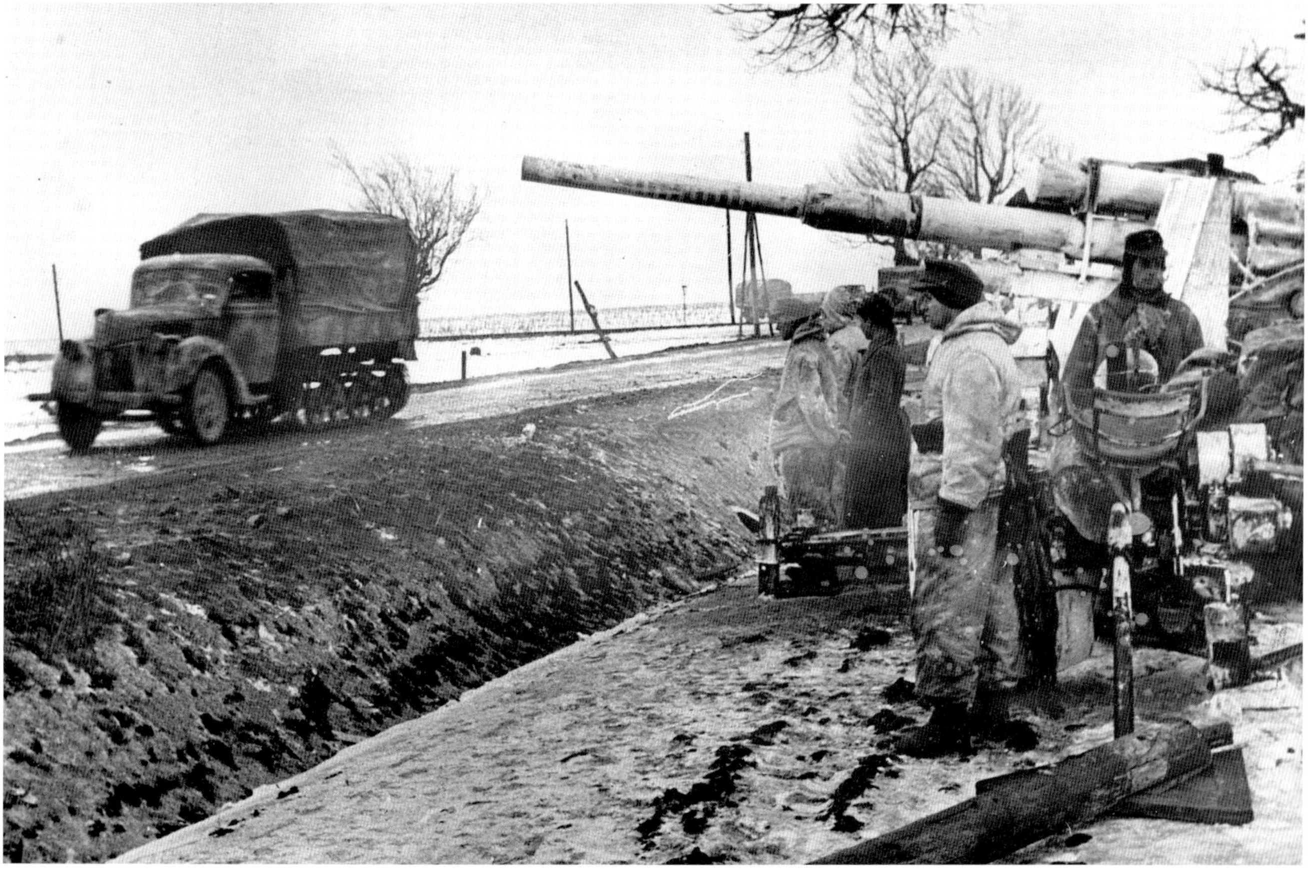

(**Opposite, above**) A variety of armoured vehicles comprising of a Panzerkampfwagen IV, Sd.Kfz.251 halftracks, support vehicles and a light Horch cross-country vehicle roll through a Belgian village.

(**Opposite, below**) During the Ardennes operation a Maultier or Sd.Kfz.3 support vehicle drives along a road passing a well positioned 8.8cm FlaK gun position. The 8.8cm FlaK gun was often difficult to make out at long-distances, especially when the crew whitewashed the weapon, which blended well with the winter surroundings. The gun fired a 9.4kg projectile, and its high velocity and flat trajectory made it a very accurate and effective weapon in both antitank and anti-aircraft roles.

(**Above**) A Panther V Ausf.G rolls along a snowy road during the Ardennes operation in late 1944. The continuous fighting in the Western Front gradually took its toll on tracks and other moving parts of the Panther, and those that were left fought a desperate defensive action all the way into Germany.

Chapter Three

Defending the Rhine

By the end of January 1945, the military situation on the Western Front was tactically in a more dangerous position than it had ever been before. The front was badly scarred and depleted and the bulk of its forces had withdrawn from Belgium and Holland and were preparing the defence of the River Rhine. Over the coming weeks fighting raged with unabated ferocity as German and Allied troops waged an unprecedented battle of attrition.

The Allies were determined to undertake a series of offensive operations designed to seize and capture the east and west bank of the Rhine. Every German soldier defending the area was aware of the significance of the Rhine being breached. Hitler made it quite clear that all remaining Wehrmacht, Waffen-SS, Luftwaffe personnel, Hitlerjugend, and Volkssturm were not to withdraw, but to stand and fight in the defensive action. He was determined not to allow the Allies to spill across the river into the heart of Germany. The ordinary German soldier knew, like all those defending the Fatherland that they were fighting now to defend their homes and loved ones.

In order to delay the Allies from crossing the Rhine the Germans flooded the Ruhr Valley by destroying the floodgates of the two dams on the upper Ruhr. This allowed units to cross the river and construct defences. It was here along the Rhine the Germans feverishly began building a maze of trenches and other defensive positions. Towns that fell in the path of these defensive belts were evacuated. Thousands of women, children and old men were removed from their dwellings and some were actually pressed into service to help construct anti-tank trenches and other obstacles.

A typical strongpoint deployed along the river and steeped back for about a mile inland comprised light and heavy MG34 and MG42 machine guns, an anti-tank rifle company or battalion, a sapper platoon that was equipped with a host of various explosives and infantry guns, an anti-tank artillery company which had a number of anti-tank guns and occasionally a self-propelled gun.

Operating at intervals were a few Pz.Kpfw IVs, Tigers, Panther tanks, and a number of StuG.III assault guns, all of which were scrapped together. This frontline defensive belt was designated as a killing zone where every possible anti-tank weapon and artillery piece would be used to ambush Allied vehicles and tanks. While an enemy tank was subjected to a storm of fire within the kill zone, special engineer mobile detachments equipped with anti-personnel and anti-tank mines would quickly deploy and erect new obstacles, just in case other tanks managed to escape the zone.

If the crew from a disabled tank had survived the initial attack and bailed out, special sapper units were ordered to pick off the unwary.

Behind these defensive positions at varying depths were anti-tank defences including mortars, Panzerschreck, Panzerfaust, 7.5cm and 8.8cm PaK guns, ready to counter any enemy armoured vehicle that managed to break through.

However, while it appeared that the Germans were prepared for the Allies, much of the equipment employed along the defensive belts was too thinly spread. Commanders too were unable to predict exactly where the strategic focal point of the attacks along the Rhine would take place. For almost two weeks the German defenders waited for the Allies to unleash their might. When the flooded area of the Ruhr Valley eventually subsided the attack began with the Allies heavily bombing German positions, severely weakening the strongest defensive lines. By 23 February the US 9th Army began its attack across the Ruhr, with other Allied forces supporting the attack from the west bank. German divisions which remained on the west bank, as the first line of the river defence, were smashed to pieces and some 280,000 soldiers taken prisoner.

On the east side of the River the Volkssturm and Hitlerjugend, many going into action for the first time, were ordered to fight fanatically to the last man. However, under-armed and under-trained, these soldiers were quickly driven from their meagre defensive positions and decimated. When some determined units refused to budge, the Allies ordered in their flame-throwers to burn them out.

Fighting along the Rhine was bitter and bloody, but with communications severed, German forces were now largely faced with either a prospect of being killed or taken prisoner. Amidst heavy unrelenting fighting, German units had no other choice than to pull back from the Rhine in a drastic attempt to escape being cut-off. Everywhere it seemed the Germans were being constantly forced to retreat. Many isolated units spent hours or even days fighting a bloody defence, but were pushed back by the enemy. As they slowly withdrew the Allies began crossing the Rhine at four points. One crossing was at the Ludendorff Bridge at Remagen when the Germans failed to blow up the bridge. This became a major crossing point. The other crossing which was undertaken on 22 and 23 March south of Mainz at Oppenheim was a hurried assault, while the other two crossings were planned at Rees and Wesel on the night of 23/24 March. The crossing was supported by the largest single-drop airborne operation in history, code-named Operation Varsity.

Following the successful crossing of the Rhine, the Allies were able to wrench open the front and begin their drive into the heartland of Germany. As for the German defenders, they were now to embark on the final defence of the Fatherland, slowly withdrawing eastwards from one fixed position to another.

(**Above**) On the Western Front in early January 1945 showing a StuG.III Ausf.G. Note on the far right, stenciled on the back plate of the vehicle, is the tactical sign for a tracked self-propelled Panzerjäger unit. Of interest is a dispatch-rider's motorcycle stowed on the near track-guard.

(**Opposite, above**) A battery of Hummels on a road bound for the front. This was a self-propelled artillery vehicle with an open-topped, lightly armoured fighting compartment at the rear of the vehicle which housed the gun and the crew. The engine had been moved to the centre of the vehicle to make room for this compartment. Later variant model Hummels had a slightly redesigned driver compartment and front superstructure in order to allow additional room for the radio operator and driver.

(**Opposite, below**) A Tiger tank rolls across a bridge laden with Fallschirmjäger troops onboard, bound for the front. This was one of the quickest forms of transporting troops from one part of the front to another where they could quickly disembark and engage the enemy.

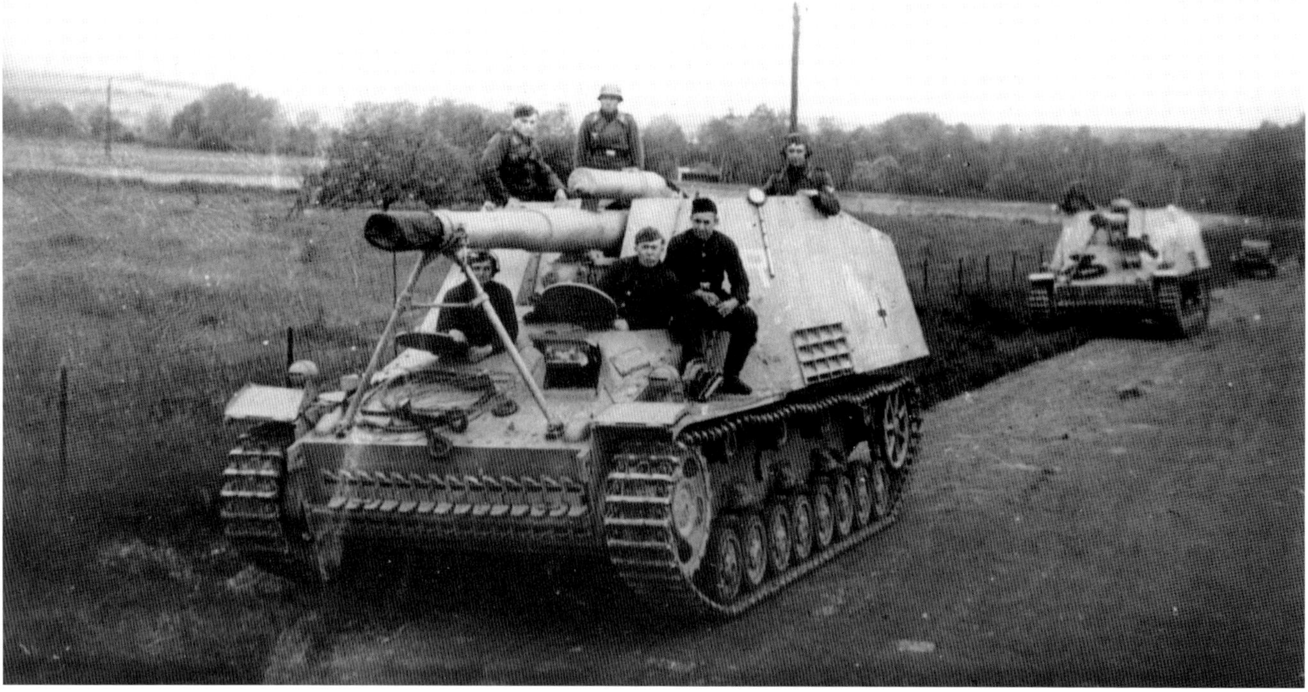

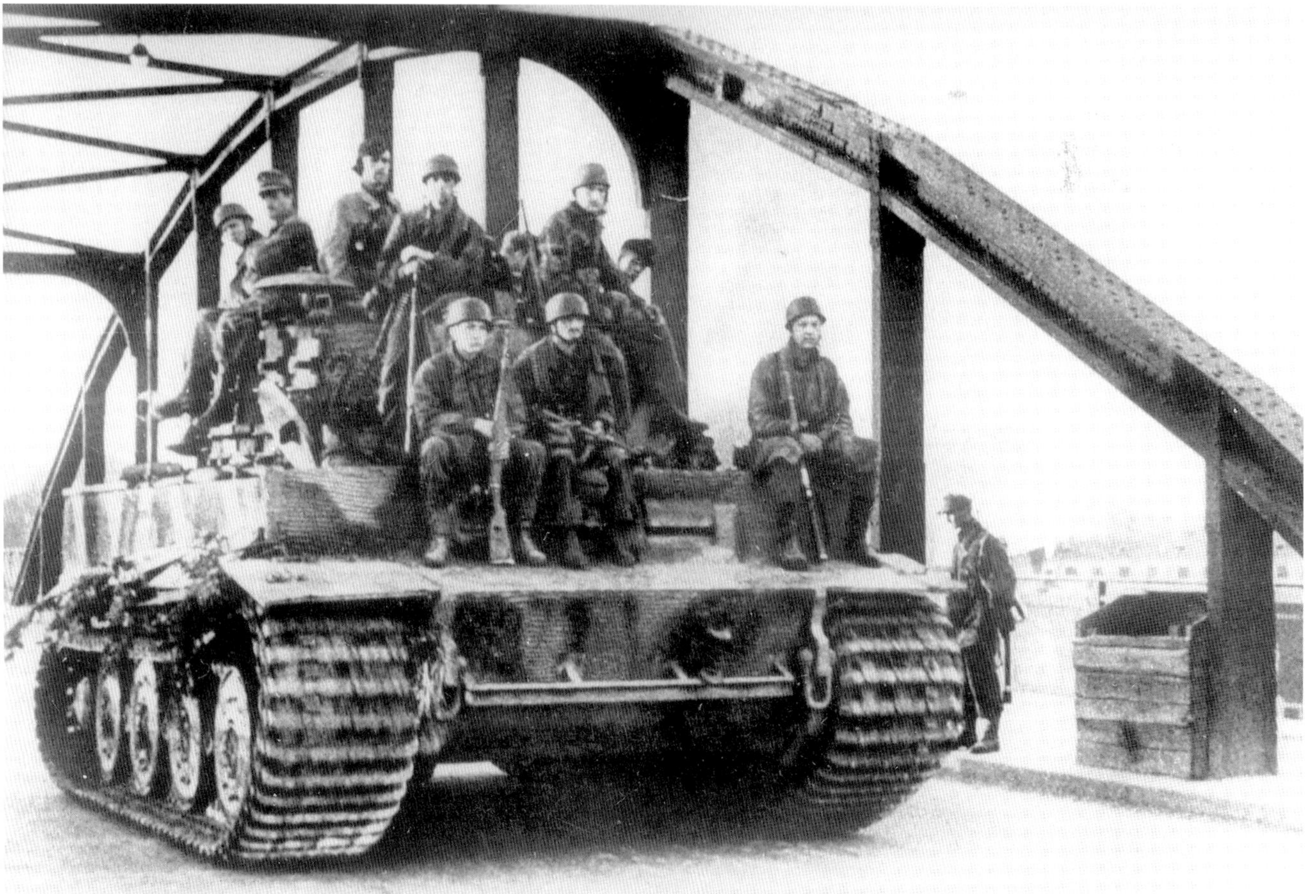

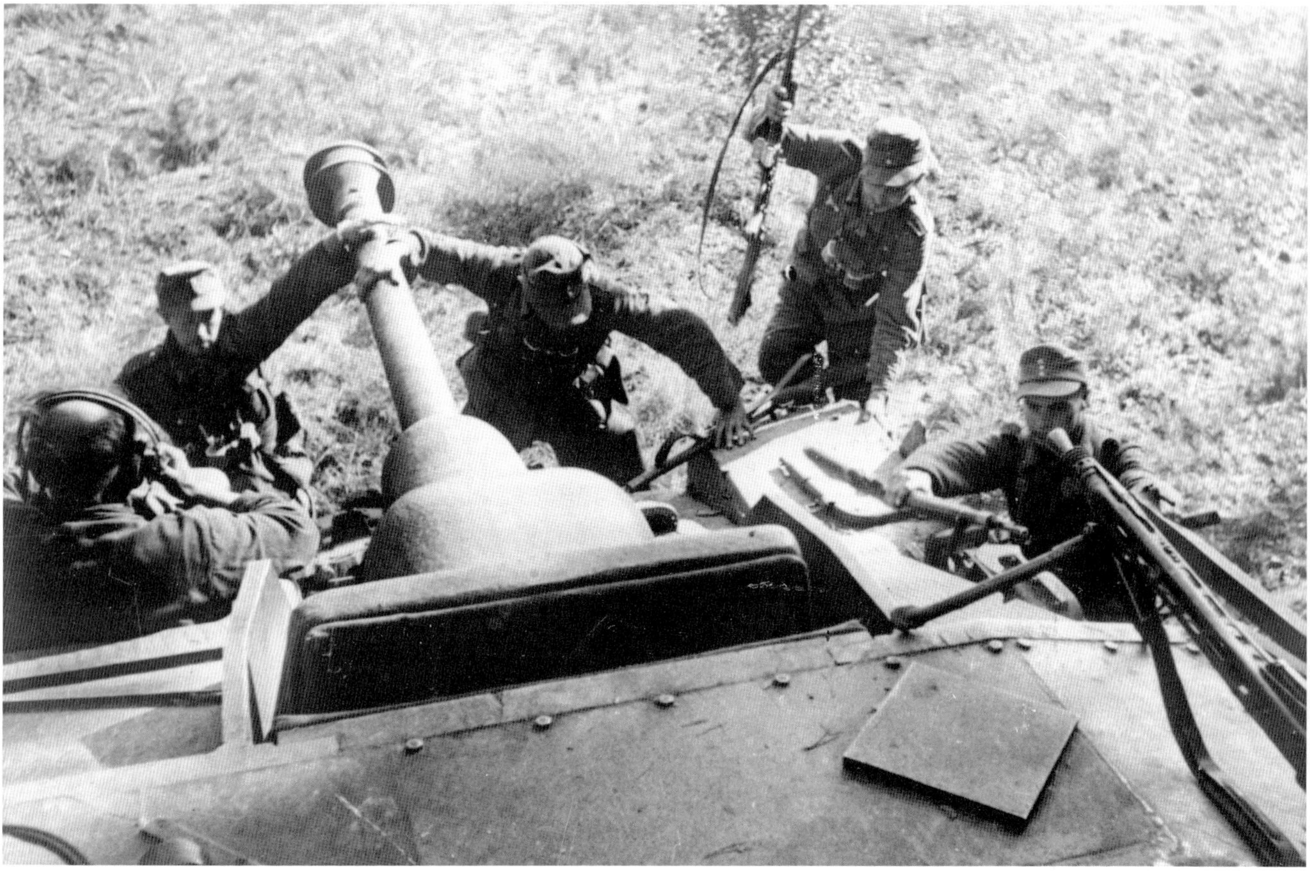

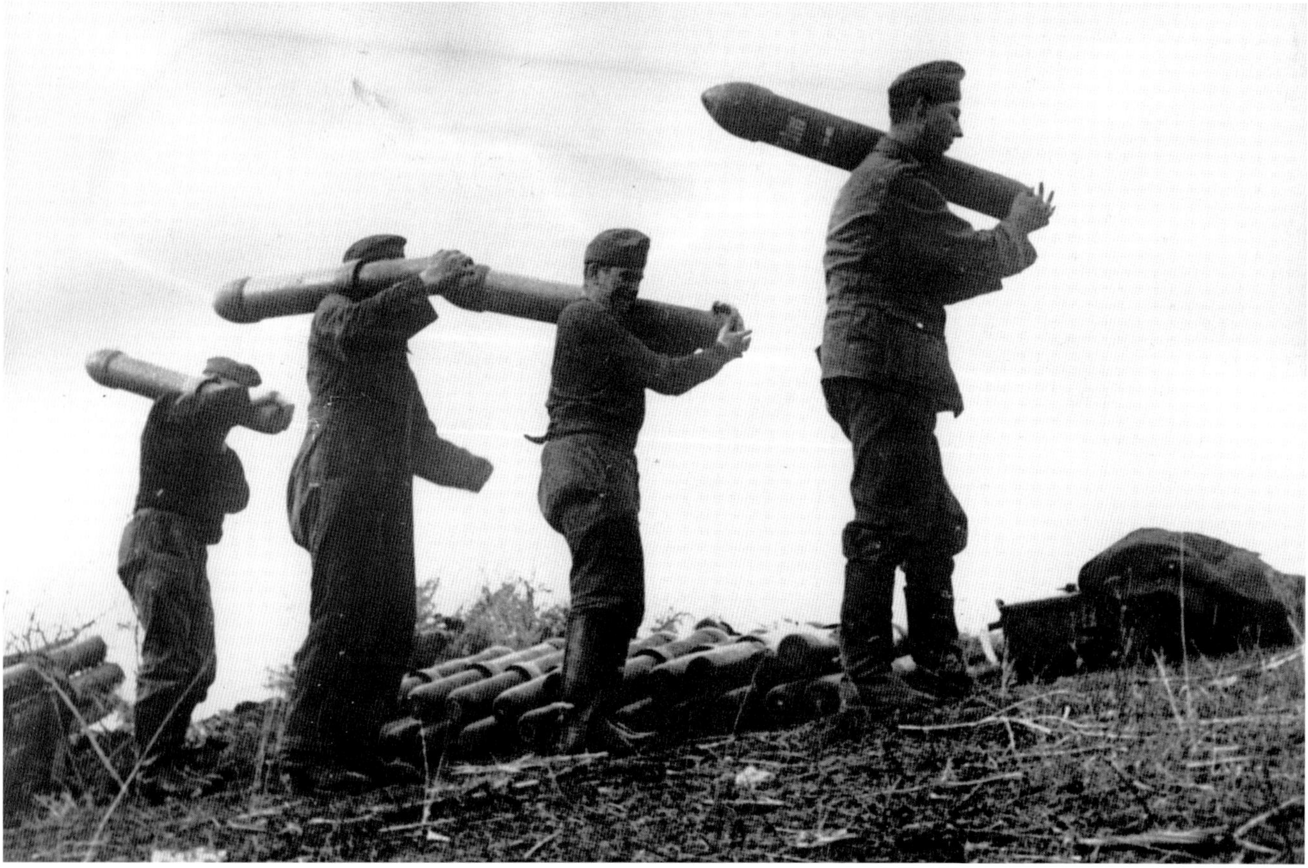

This dug-in 8.8cm FlaK with hand-applied camouflage pattern is engaged in firing against an enemy target. Note the pneumatic recuperator cylinders which have been given added splinted protection, using what are probably wooden beams.

(**Opposite, above**) A Sturmgeschütz self-propelled crew about to climb onboard their StuG.III Ausf.G during operations on the Western Front. Note the MG42 with bipod extended on the roof plate of the vehicle.

(**Opposite, below**) Part of a Nebelwerfer unit transporting on their shoulders one of the rocket projectiles for the Nebelwerfer rocket launchers. Initially, Nebeltruppen were organised into six batteries of six or eight rocket launchers, three batteries per battalion. Later in the war Nebeltruppen were simply referred to as Werfer and regiments were often reinforced with a Panzerwerfer battery of six to eight vehicles.

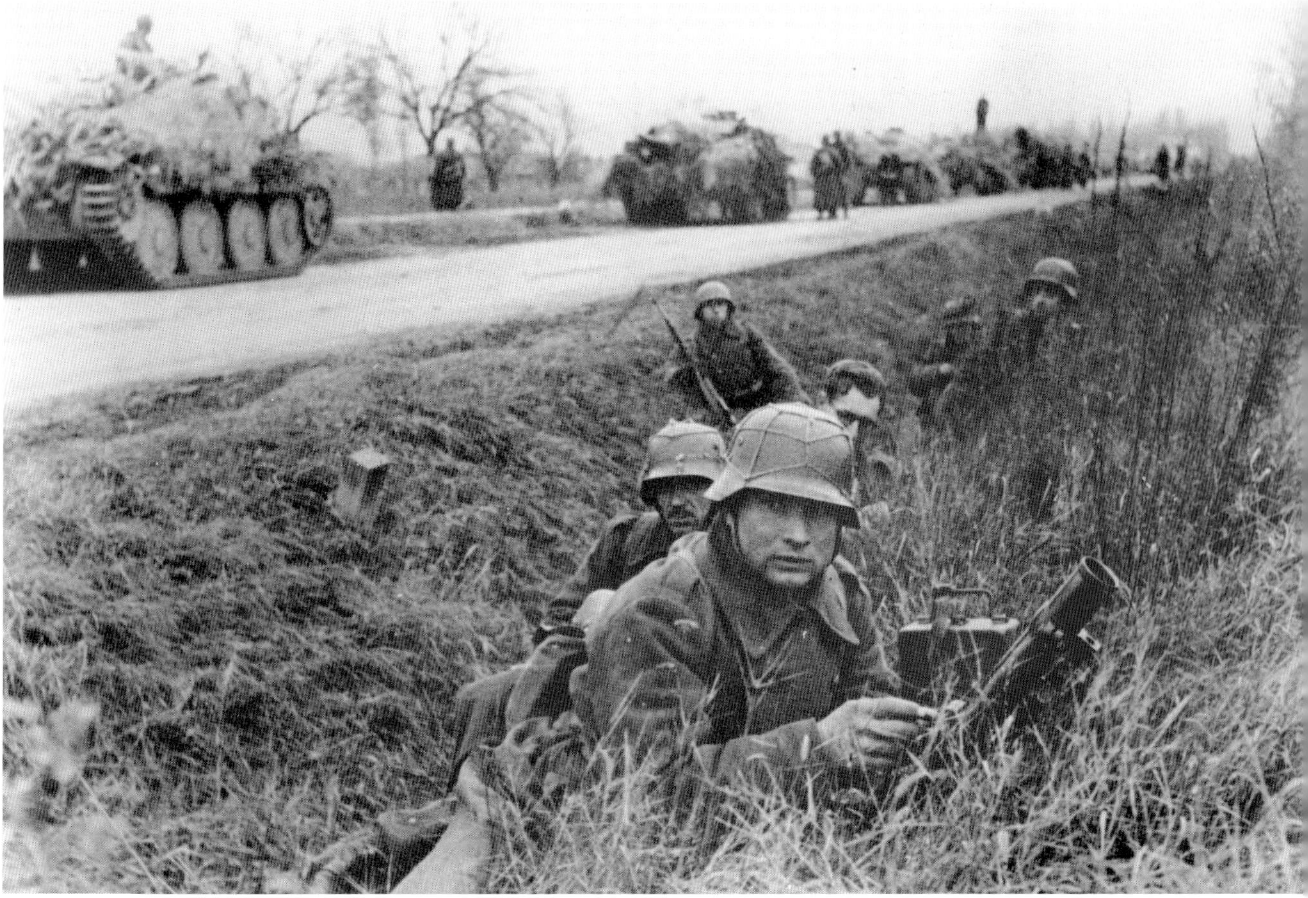

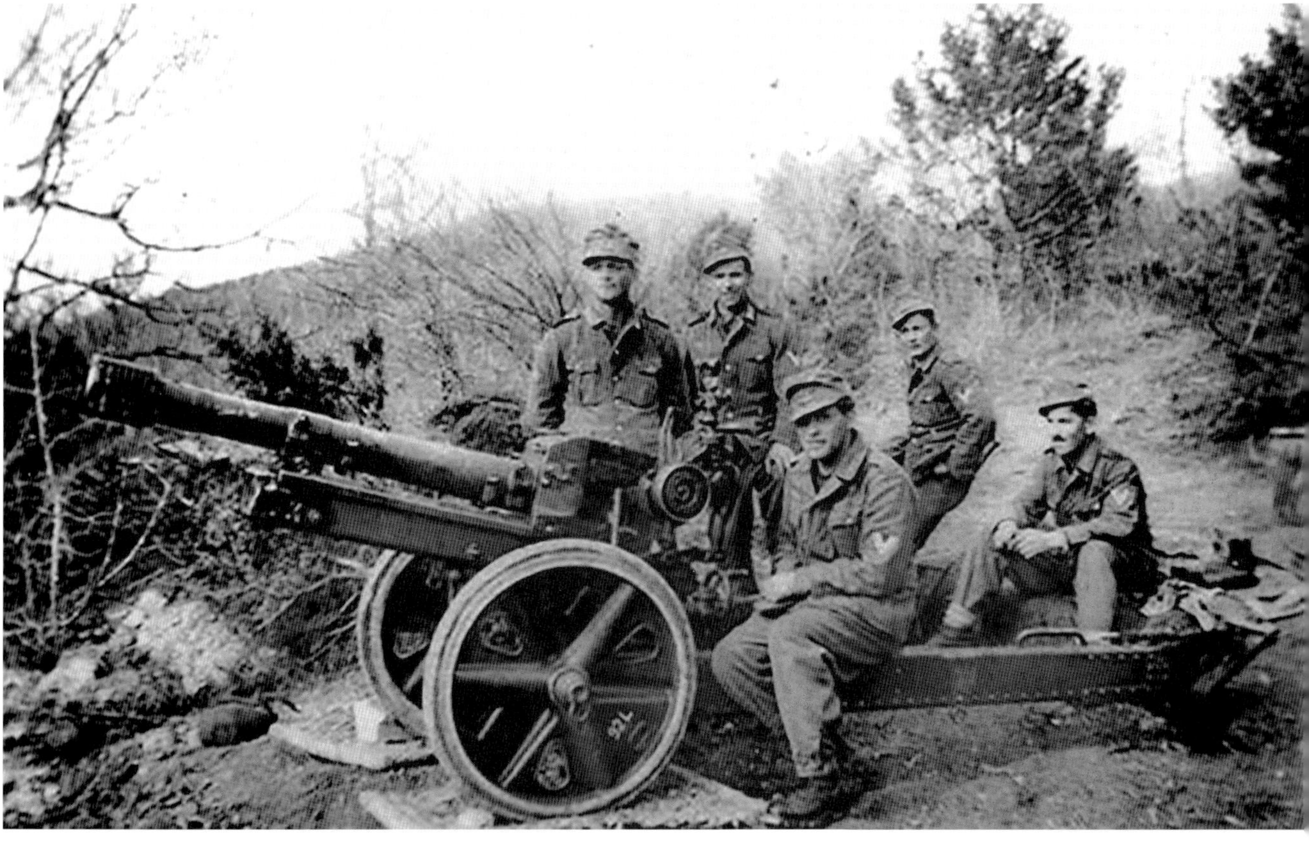

A grenadier smiles for the camera armed with the deadly Panzerfaust slung over his shoulder. During the last year of the war the Panzerfaust was used extensively to combat Russian armour. It was a handheld rocket-propelled grenade which was effective at a range of about 90 feet.

(**Opposite, above**) On a road on the Western Front is a line of Jagdpanzer 38 Hetzer tank destroyers. The vehicles have an extensive camouflage of foliage in order to disguise their shape. Sitting at the side of the road in a ditch are panzergrenadiers armed with an assortment of weapons including the 5cm Leichter Granatwerfer 36 light mortar.

(**Opposite, below**) Troops pose for the camera with the 7.5cm Gebirgsgeschütz 36 which is a 7.5cm mountain gun primarily designed for the German mountain troops or Gebirgsjäger. The gun could be broken down into eight loads for transportation.

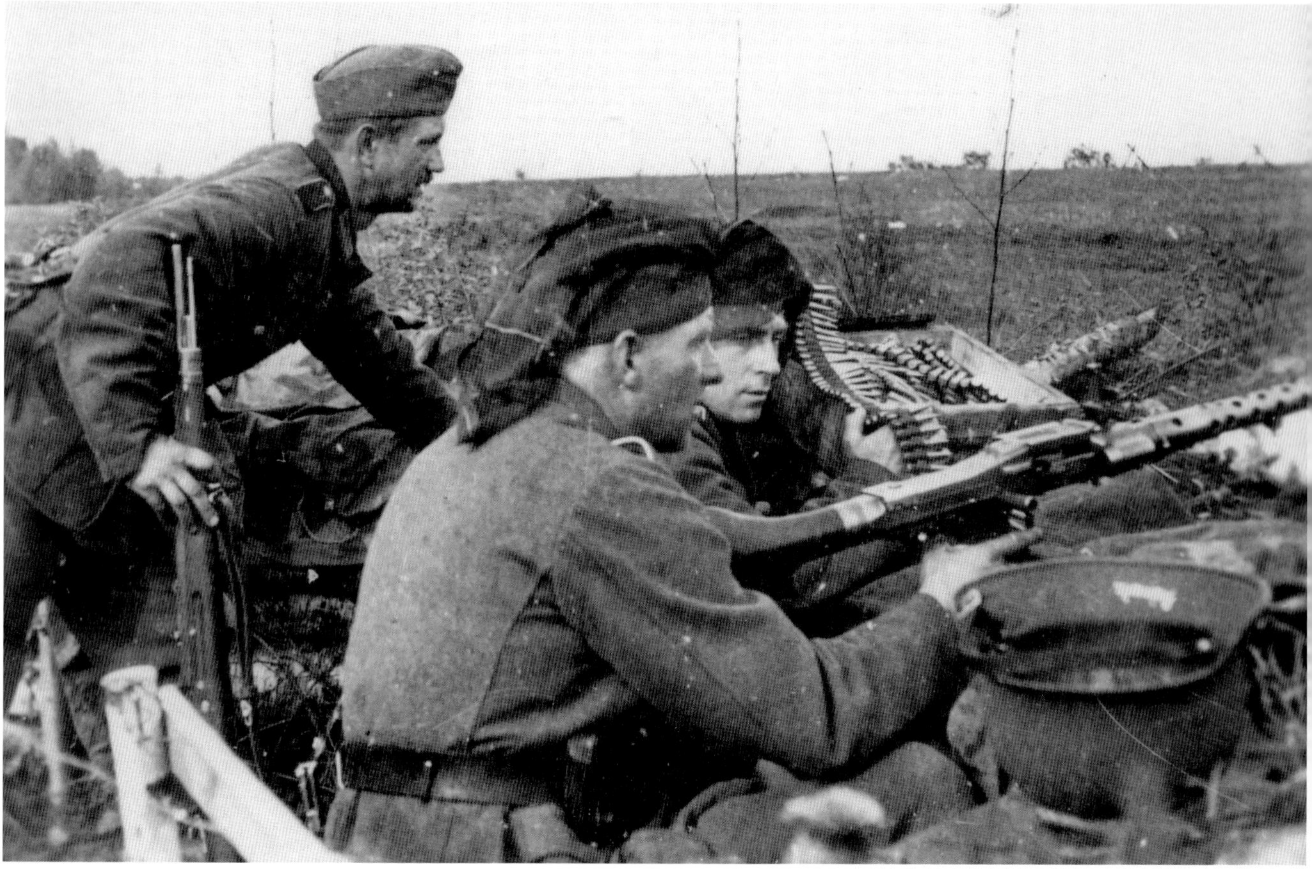

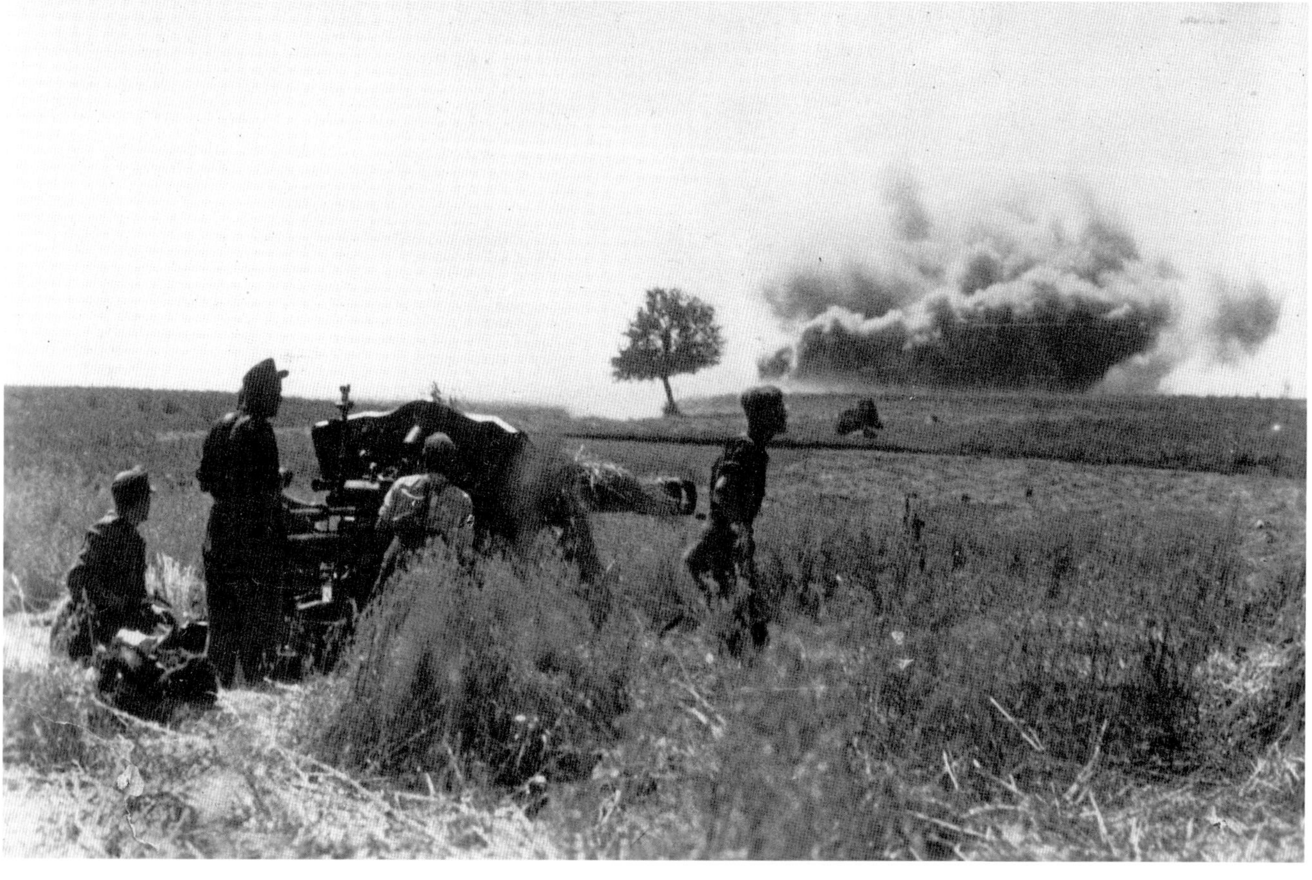

A soldier who is part of an MG42 machine gun crew marches along a road wearing his waterproof Zeltbahn shelter quarter and his MG42 machine gun bullet belt slung around his neck. He also carries a spare ammunition case.

(**Opposite, above**) In a defensive position an MG34 machine gun crew can be seen observing the terrain for enemy detection. The infantry battalion's machine gun company had two heavy machine gun platoons, each with four guns. In open terrain they would protect the flanks of advancing rifle companies, as in this photograph.

(**Opposite, below**) During defensive action on the Western Front a PaK crew can be seen in an open field. One of the crew members standing forward of the PaK 40 is trying to deduce the location of the enemy.

(**Above**) The crew of a 3.7cm FlaK gun are well dug in and stand ready to meet enemy contact. These guns performed very well during the war and were in service until 1945.

(**Opposite, above**) One of the most impressive mortars used by the Germans on both the Western and Eastern Fronts was the 12cm Granatwerfer 378(r). This weapon consisted of a circular base plate, the tube and the supporting bipod, weighing 285kg. Because of its excessive weight, a two wheeled axle was used, enabling the mortar to be towed into action. The axle could then be quickly removed before firing. The weapon fired the Wurfgranate 42 round, which carried 3.1kg of explosives. A mortar crew usually consisted of at least three members: the gunner controlled the deflection and elevation of the weapon, the assistant gunner loaded the round at the command of the gunner and the ammunition man prepared and handed over ammunition to the assistant gunner.

(**Opposite, below**) An MG42 light machine gun crew have dug in along a river during a defensive action against the Allies. When times and conditions allowed, machine gun crews invariably prepared a number of fall-back positions. They appreciated the full value of the MG42, and along these fall-back positions the machine gunners were able to set up advantageous defensive positions.

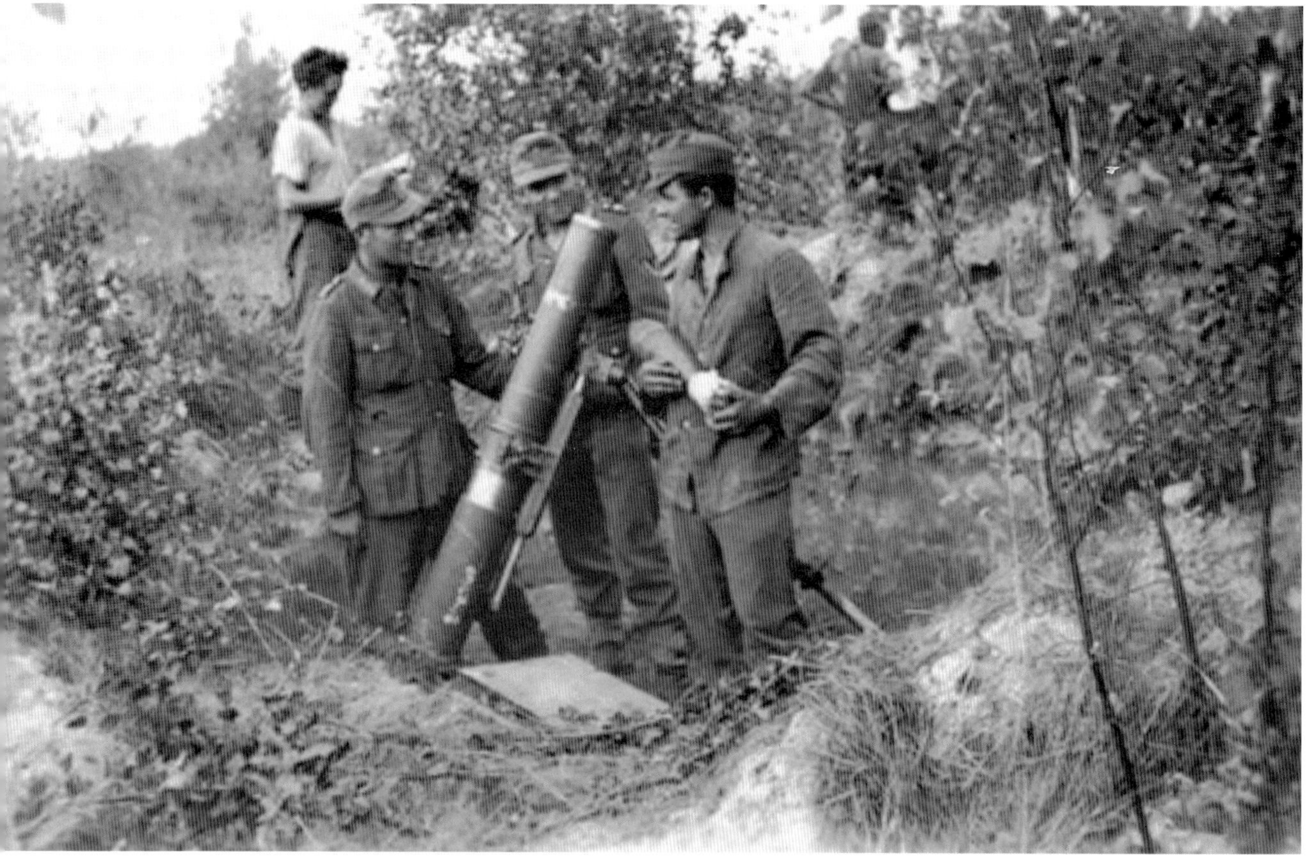

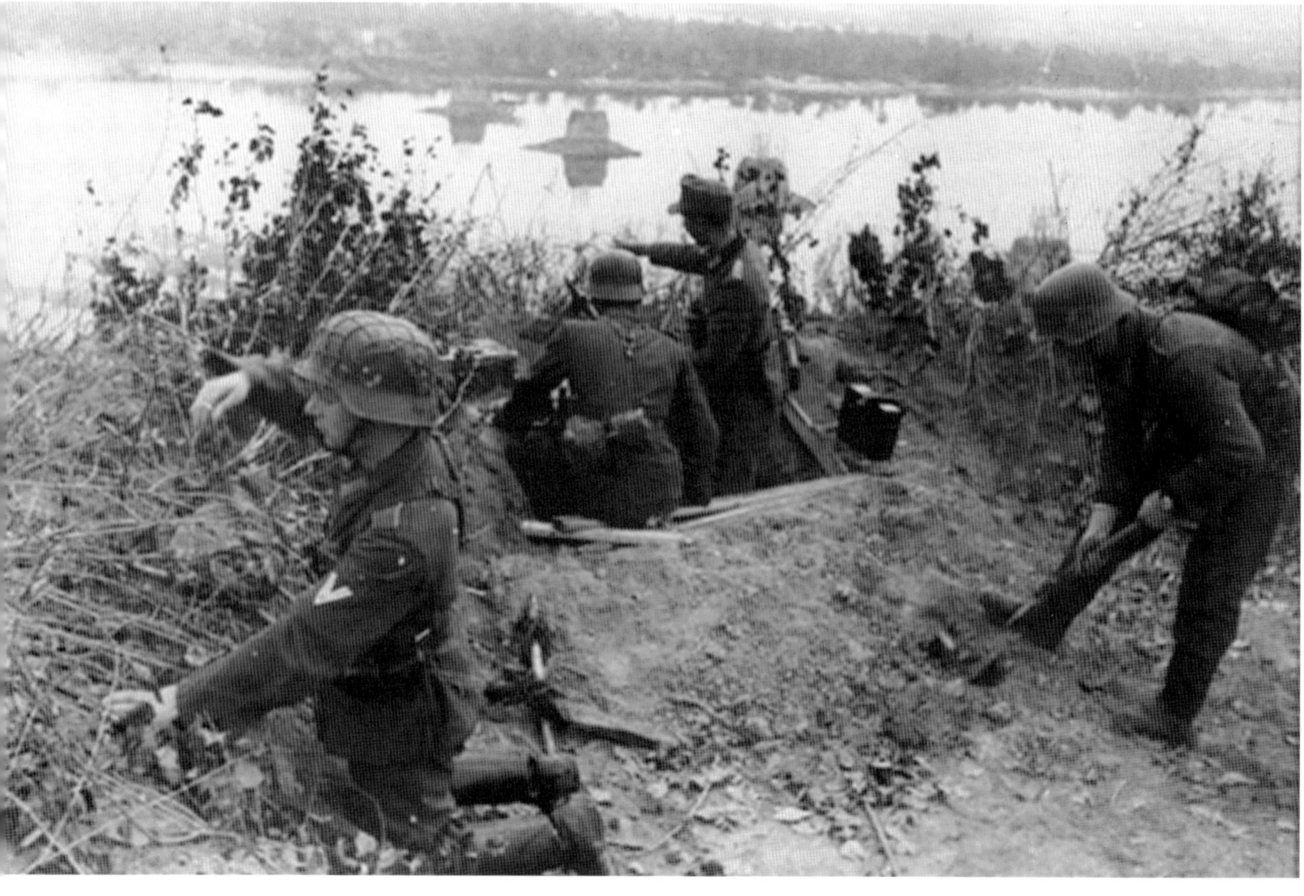

A photograph showing a heavy MG42 machine gun position on a sustained fire mount. In open terrain the MG42 machine gun squad would use their sustained fire mount to protect the flanks of advancing rifle companies. However, in built-up areas the crews often had to operate forward with the rifle platoons and in light machine gun roles with bipods only. They could still take advantage of a situation and revert back to a heavy machine gun role.

An excellent photograph showing the crew of a 7.5cm PaK 97/38 preparing their gun along a road for firing. During the last months of the war, PaK crews often prepared their guns on roads or crossroads, where they had the most advantageous position against the enemy.

The moment a 21cm Mörser 18 is being fired against an enemy target. Note the crew members plugging their ears to protect them against the loud blast.

An interesting photograph showing two soldiers servicing a Panzerschreck or tank shocker. One is holding and aiming the weapon while his comrade behind him loads the projectile. A popular name given by the troops for this weapon was the Raketenpanzerbüchse or rocket tank rifle, abbreviated to RPzB. It was an 8.8cm reusable anti-tank rocket launcher developed during the latter half of the war. Another popular nickname was Ofenrohr or stove pipe.

A photograph taken the moment a 7.5cm PaK 40 fires at an enemy target. The piece has been partly concealed by camouflage netting. Note one of the gunners plugging his ears.

Chapter Four

Last Battles in the West

German commanders in the field now resigned themselves to the gloomy prospect of losing large parts of Western Germany, and the news sent shock waves through the German High Command. For them it marked the beginning of the final defence of the Fatherland on the Western Front. As German forces fought to delay the inevitable capture of one German district after another, the main bulk of the Allied drive bypassed various pockets of resistance that were still attempting to defend areas along the Rhine, and surged into Germany where it fought a number of hard-pressed battles.

Almost continuously Allied pressure was maintained, while German commanders strove desperately to stabilise the deteriorating situation. While some areas still held fanatically a general breakdown began to sweep the German lines. Although the German soldiers were generally determined to fight, they were constantly being isolated and trapped by superior numbers of enemy infantry. Areas that still remained in German hands were slowly reduced to a few shrinking pockets of resistance. Although there were many appeals for reinforcements to the frontal sectors, there were no more reserves left in the west. Instead troops fought on with what they had left, and units that had not been encircled or tied down in bitter fighting withdrew, all attempting to get through to the main German lines that were moving eastward. As they withdrew the majority of troops were forced to abandon most of their heavy equipment and weapons. Consequently, there were frequent scenes of chaos and disorganization as they retreated along forest roads and paths trying to escape from the jaws of the Allied advance.

On 1 April 1945, German Army Group B became surrounded in the Ruhr. General Field Marshal Walter Model had been charged with the defence of the Ruhr region. Model was regarded as the Führer's troubleshooter. He had been the commander that had first introduced, in early 1944, the 'Shield and Sword' policy on the Eastern Front, which stated that retreats were intolerable, allowed only if they paved the way for a counterstroke later. Out on the battlefield Model was not only energetic, courageous and innovative, but was friendly and popular with his enlisted men. Now commander of Army Group B on the Western Front he was given the awesome task of trying to minimize the extent of the disaster in the Ruhr region.

Here he had deployed significant numbers of troops along the east-west Sieg River south of Cologne. However, Model's strategy of trying to deduce the enemies' plans saw thousands of his troops become cut off. Throughout April he tried in vain to punch a hole through the Allied lines and escape, but opposition was strong and remnants of Army Group B either continued fighting until they were annihilated or surrendered. As a result of the systematic destruction of Army Group B and Model's failure to defend the Ruhr, the General committed suicide on 21 April.

Elsewhere on the Western Front there were general collapses everywhere. The absence of communications too made it impossible for the Germans to assess the full extent of disintegration. There seemed no stopping the tide of the Allied advance, and as they remorselessly pushed forward German formations became increasingly confused and entangled in bitter bloody fighting.

On 9 April, the US 12th Army reached the River Elbe which had been the American's furthest eastward objective. Berlin seemed to be within its grasp as units began making a dash toward Magdeburg, just 50 miles from the Reich capital. On 12 April, additional elements of the US 9th Army had reached the Elbe, crushed most of the German resistance along the river line and then crossed to the opposite bank.

As the Allies pushed forward they were once again met with stiff resistance. In and around the city of Leipzig, German defence was considerably strong comprising of anti-tank defences, mines, and an assortment of barricades with a number of other bunker installations and forts. Outside Leipzig along the Mulde River the Germans had also dug-in and were determined not to surrender. Here along the river it was defended by a mixture of infantry, Panzertruppen, Volkssturm and Hitlerjugend. Although the Germans were poorly matched in terms of equipment and supply, a number of the troops were hardened veterans that had survived some of the most costly battles on the Western Front. Hurriedly these troops were positioned along the main roads leading east. Heavy machine gun platoons dug in and held each end of the line while the remainder were scattered in various buildings, trenches and dug-outs. Remaining armoured vehicles took up key positions in order to defend the main lines. Crude obstacles were erected and troops were emplaced in defensive positions armed with a motley assortment of anti-tank and FlaK guns, machine guns, Panzerfaust and the deadly Panzerschreck. Yet, through a combination of wide flanking operations the Americans managed to bypass much of the German defensive positions along the river and advance on Leipzig. Even though defence of the city was fierce, superior American strength soon overwhelmed the defenders. German commanders were all too aware of the significant strength of their resilient foe and hoped that they could contain them for as long as possible. However, the attack through the city was swift and it was captured on 20 April.

Elsewhere on the Western Front, the situation for the Germans was just as bleak. Canadian forces had reached the North Sea near the Dutch border and driven through the central Netherlands, trapping what was left of the German forces defending the country.

On 25 April, Soviet and American forces met at the Elbe River near Torgau in Germany, With this contact between the Soviets advancing from the East and the Americans advancing from the West, the Reich had effectively been cut in two. The Russians were now to swing round north-eastwards towards Berlin to meet the main Soviet assault on the decimated Reich capital. As for the Allies, they were not interested in a long protracted battle for Berlin where thousands of lives would be lost. Instead, they left the city to the Russians while they ordered American forces into the south of Germany to cut off and wipe out the last remnants of the Wehrmacht. In the north of the country, the British continued undertaking similar operations.

Although by May 1945 the war was over, there were numerous groupings of uncaptured German soldiers, Hitlerjugend and Volkssturm, some dressed in civilian clothes, that fanatically continued resisting. However, these too were eventually killed or captured, ending the German defence on the Western Front forever.

Panzerfaust patrol in the winter of 1945. They wear a variety of winter garments comprising the standard issue Wehrmacht greatcoat, white insulated suits and Wehrmacht splinter jackets.

An SS grenadier, wearing a camouflaged two-piece reversible winter suit, sits inside a Volkswagen Schwimmwagen during reconnaissance operations on the Western Front.

During the latter part of the war divisional cyclist and reconnaissance battalions were reorganised and redesignated as division fusilier battalions. They served as a mobile reserve with reconnaissance, and most were equipped with bicycles to provide mobility, and were surprisingly heavily armoured. In this photograph these fusiliers are armed with two Panzerfaust anti-tank projectors fitted on their troop bicycles. The bicycles were painted field grey or black and the Panzerfaust was painted in dark tan yellow.

An interesting image showing a mortar crew posing for the camera wearing the standard Wehrmacht greatcoats and two-piece insulated winter uniforms. The mortar is the deadly 12cm Granatwerfer 378(r). These large mortars were a drastic attempt to give German infantry units in the latter part of the war close support with a much greater performance than the mortars already in service at the time.

(**Above**) Young grenadiers in their Wehrmacht greatcoats armed with the Panzerfaust anti-tank projectors march through a German town during the defence of the Reich in 1945. They are laden with a full kit and also armed with Karabiner 98K bolt action rifle.

(**Opposite, above**) An Sd.Kfz.251 halftrack communication vehicle fitted with additional radio equipment for command use crosses a field during a reconnaissance mission during the latter part of the war.

(**Opposite, below**) An Sd.Kfz.251 halted out in the field. Grenadiers are supporting the march and can be seen armed with a variety of weapons including the Karabiner 98K and MG42. Note one soldier carrying the bipod for the 8cm Granatwerfer 34 mortar. These mortars were of conventional design and broke down for transport into three loads (smooth bore barrel, bipod, baseplate).

An interesting photograph showing an Sd.Kfz.10/5 parked alongside a road. This is the unarmoured version mounting the 2cm FlaK 38, although the identifying feature was not the gun, but the width of the platform. These vehicles were issued to independent anti-aircraft battalions in both the Heer and Luftwaffe.

Nebeltruppen are seen here connecting their Nebelwerfer projectile weapon to the rear of an artillery tractor. In the latter part of the war these Nebeltruppen were redesignated as Volks-Werfer brigades.

Grenadiers carrying parts of a Panzerschreck march through a wooded area. During the latter parts of the war Panzerschreck and Panzerfaust teams were used into strong defensive positions and deployed into staggered trenches where they were ordered to attack advancing Allied armour.

(**Above**) Two Sd.Kfz.251 halftracks have halted along a road. Grenadiers have hitched a lift onboard these vehicles so at a moment's notice they could dismount. For the troops this was the most effective and quickest way of being transported either to the battlefield, or being withdrawn to another line of defence. When the halftracks arrived at the edge of a battlefield, the troops were able to quickly dismount and take up positions.

(**Opposite, above**) Concealed in the undergrowth is a FlaK gunner sitting in the chair of a 2cm FlaK 30 anti-aircraft gun. The gun is attached to its Sd.Ah.51 trailer. By using it in this configuration the gun could be fired quickly in an emergency.

(**Opposite, below**) A Tiger tank halted on a road inside a devastated German town. By the latter stages of the war the Tiger tank was among the number of armoured vehicles stretched all too thinly along the Western Front. Panzer divisions too were often broken up and split among hastily constructed battle groups or Kampfgruppe drawn from a motley collection of armoured formations. These battle groups were put into the line operating well below strength. The demands that were put upon the Panzerwaffe during the last year of the war were immeasurable. The constant employment and the nightmare of not having enough supplies worried the commanders constantly. The Allies, encouraged by the Germans dire situation, now mounted bolder operations aimed directly at the German front.

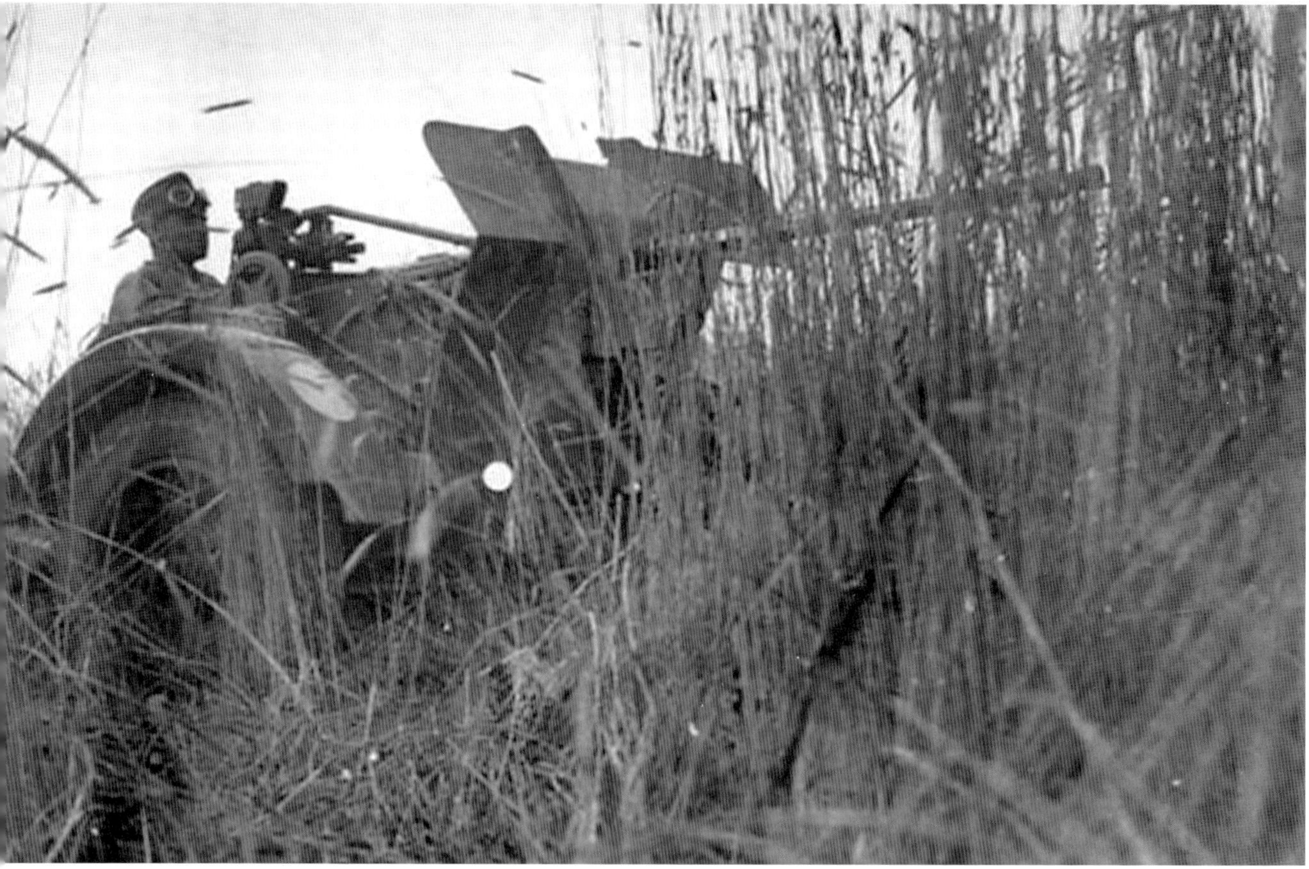

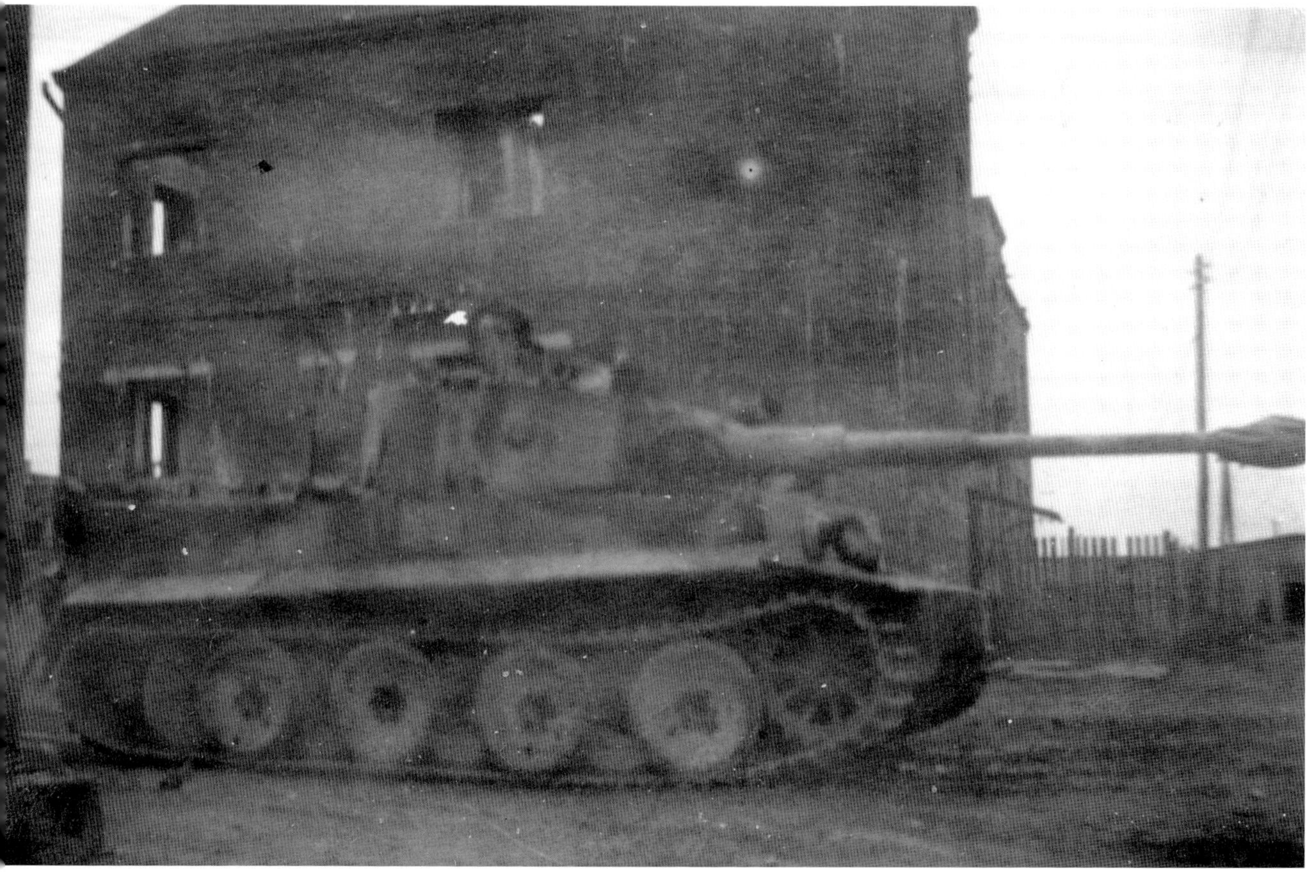

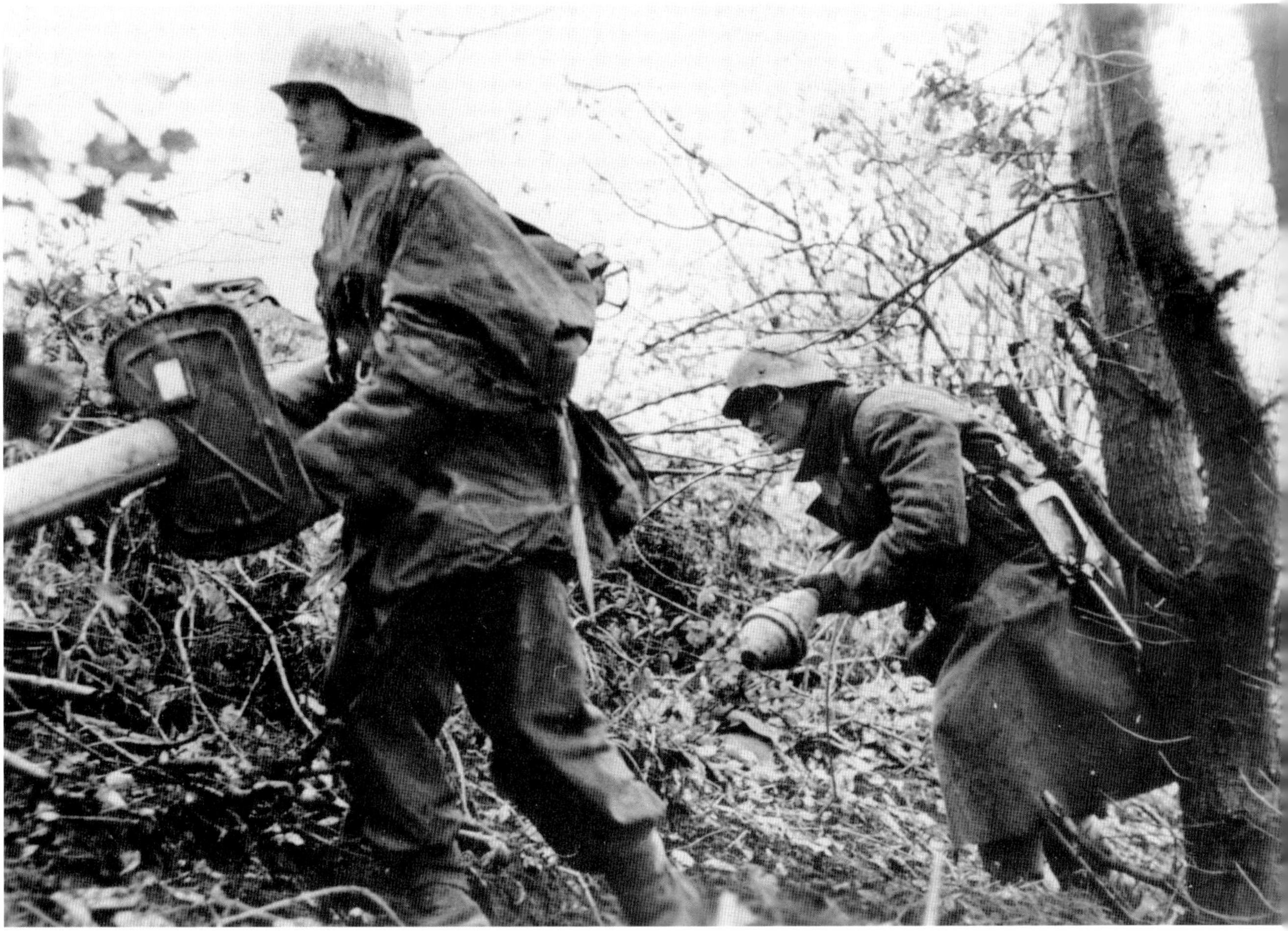

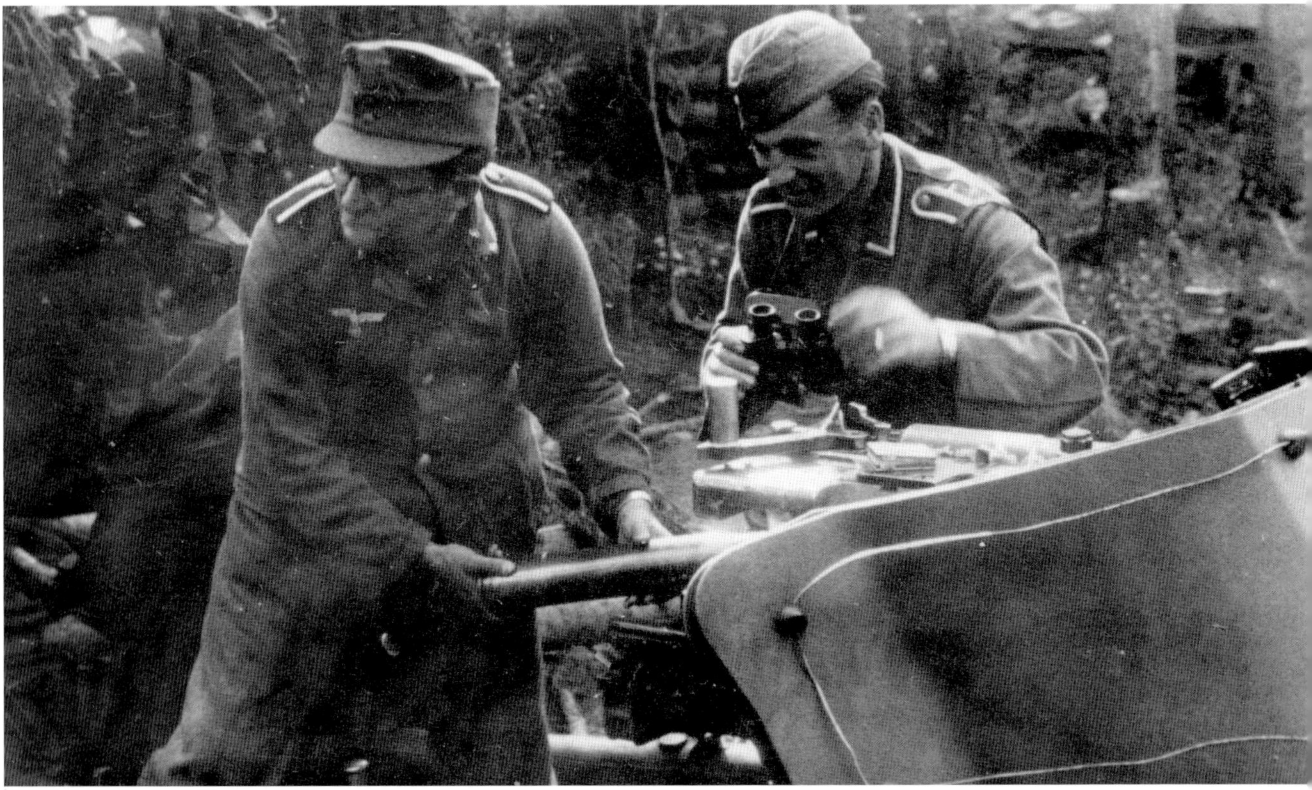

A Wehrmacht recruit given a quick lesson in the use of the Panzerfaust. By 1945 there was a dramatic increase in the loss of Allied tanks to the Panzerfaust, and more than half of the tanks knocked out in combat were destroyed by Panzerfaust or Panzerschreck.

(**Opposite, above**) Grenadiers moving stealthily through undergrowth, one armed with the Panzerschreck and the other the Panzerfaust. It was often down to these men, armed with these weapons, to defend towns and villages from the onrushing Allied forces.

(**Opposite, below**) PaK gunners preparing their weapons for action against an enemy target.

(**Above**) On the march are grenadiers. Note one of them armed with the Panzerfaust. This weapon comprised a small, disposable preloaded launch tube firing a high explosive anti-tank warhead, operated by a single soldier. The Panzerfaust remained in service in various versions until the end of the war. The weapon often had warnings, written in large red letters on the upper rear end of the tube, advising the user of the back blast.

(**Opposite, above**) A photograph of a soldier using a 4 × Zeiss ZF42 telescopic sight on a Karabiner 98K bolt action rifle. The 98K with a telescopic sight was a very accurate weapon and had an effective range of up to 1,000 metres when used by a well seasoned sniper.

(**Opposite, below**) Two grenadiers assemble to commence their march. They are armed with the Panzerfaust 30 anti-tank projectors. Behind them is a halted Sd.Kfz.251 halftrack that has been fully applied with foliage.

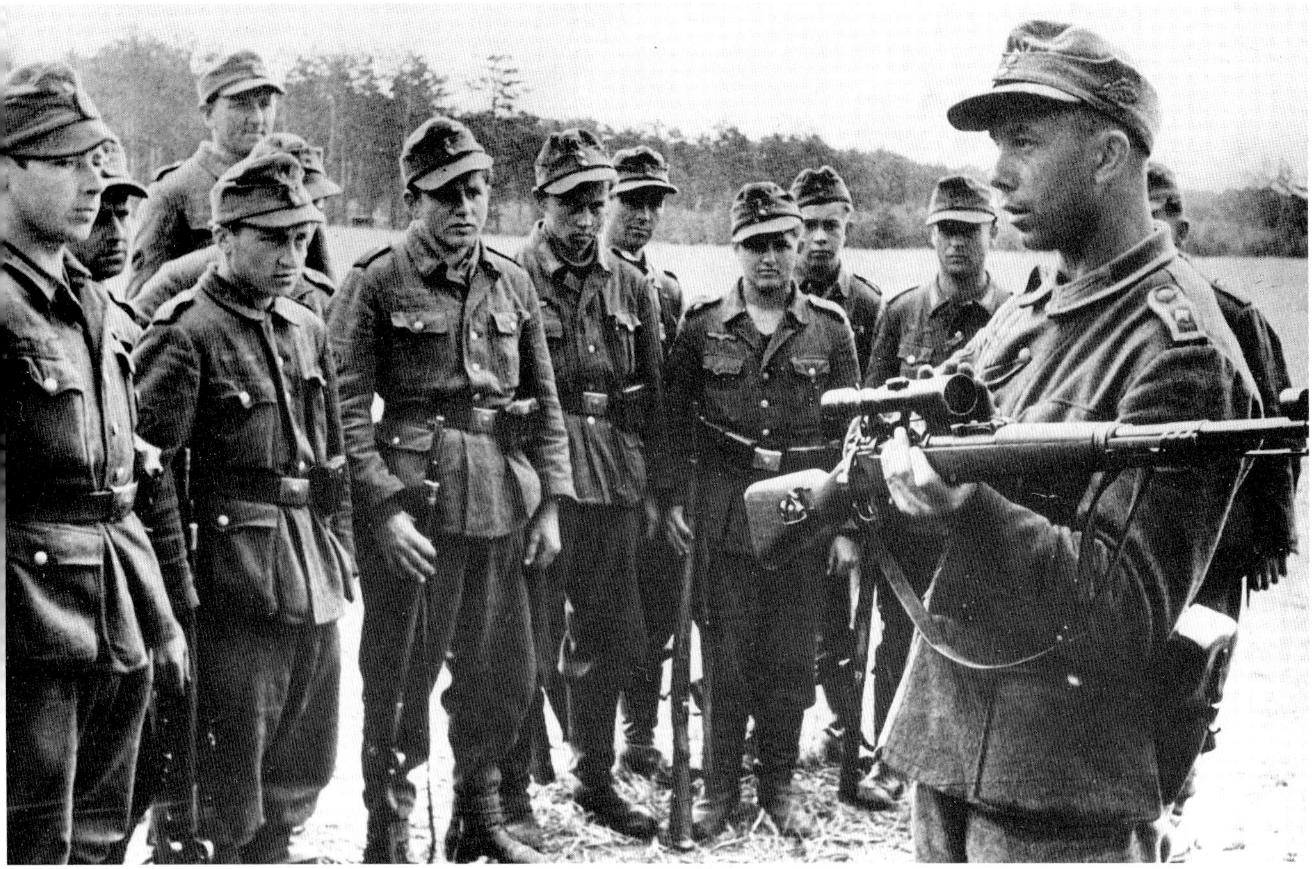

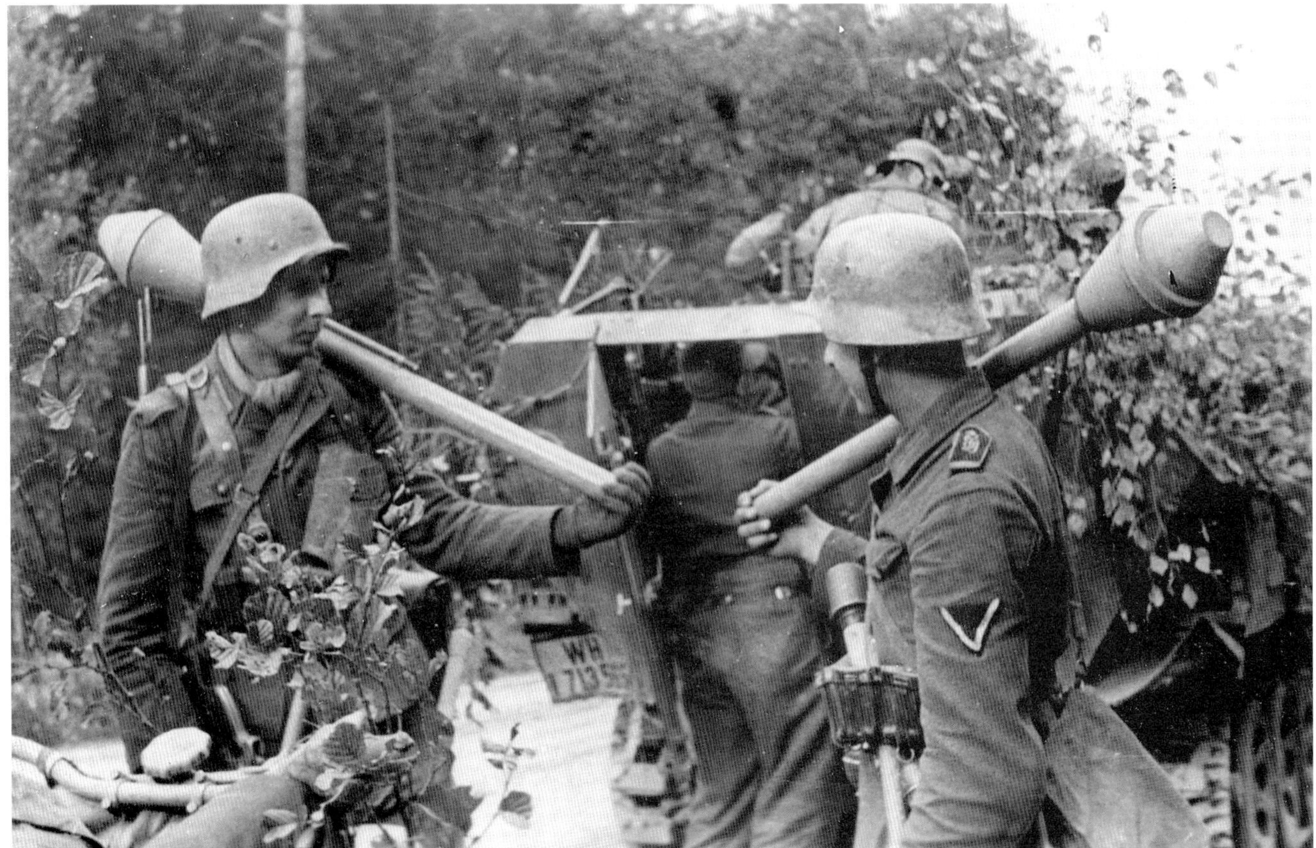
WH

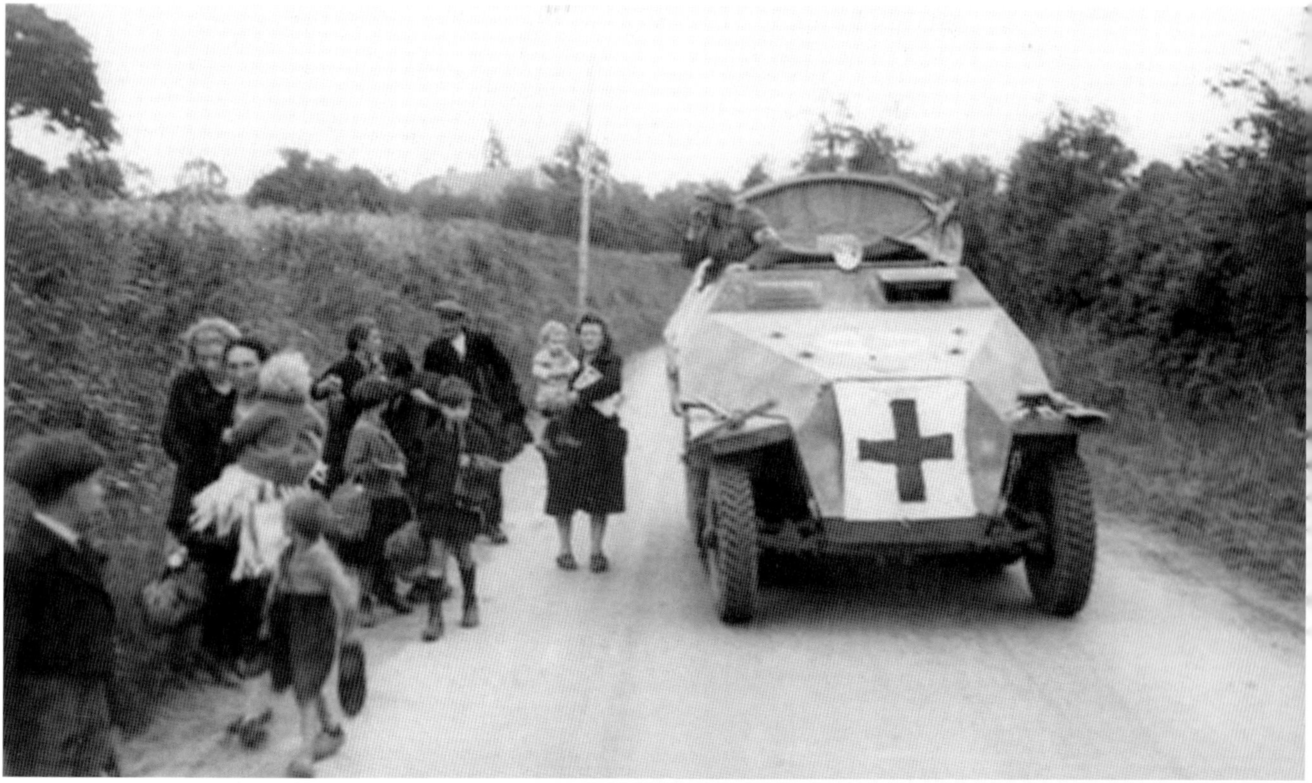

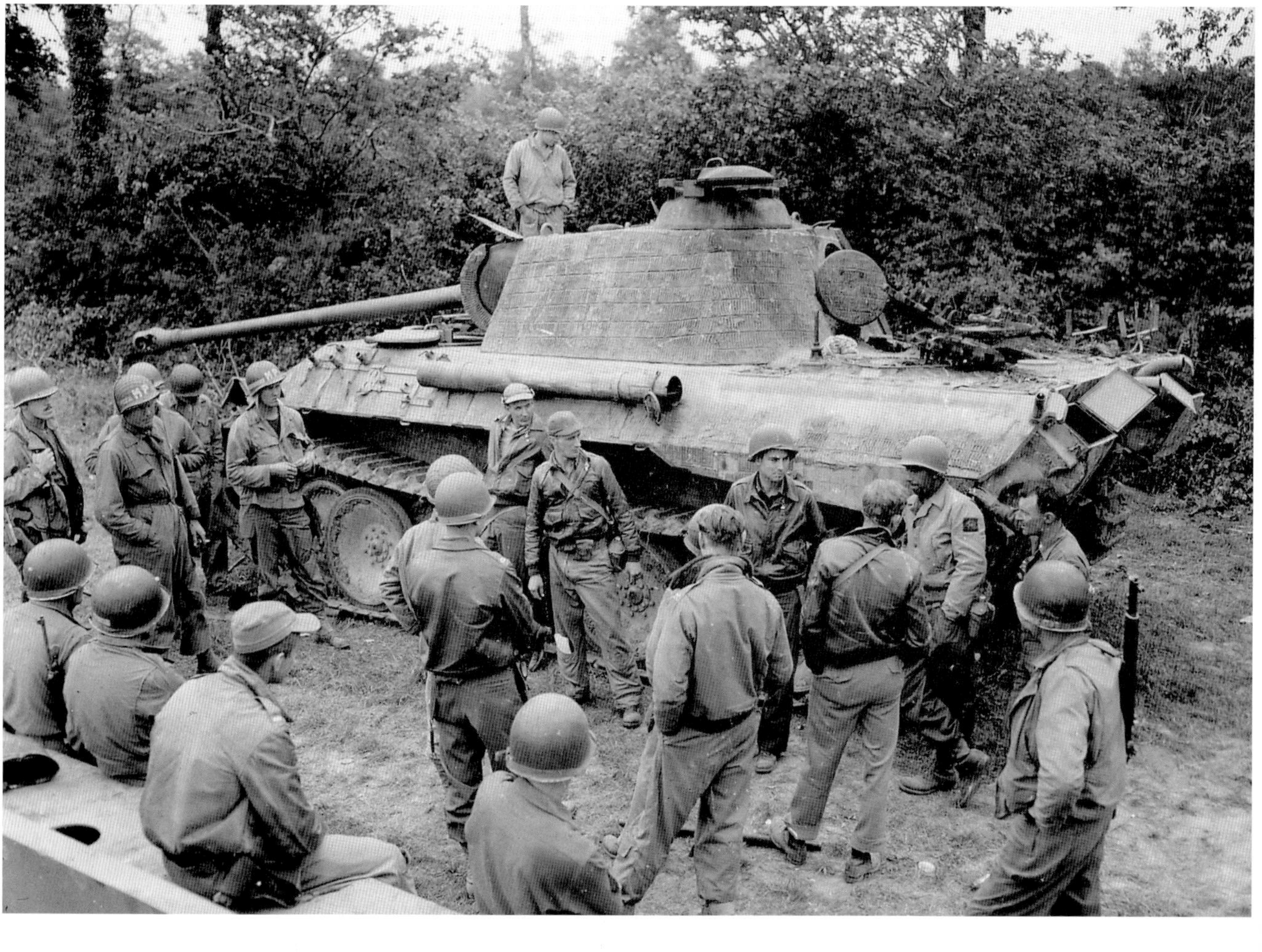
MP

(**Opposite, above**) An Sd.Kfz.251/8 displaying a red cross marking on the front plate of the vehicle indicating it is an armoured ambulance. One of the crewman can be seen calling out to the refugees on foot walking along a road.

(**Opposite, below**) American troops can be seen with a knocked out Panther Ausf.A. The Panzer is coated in Zimmerit anti-magnetic mine paste. Note the tanks long L/70 gun tube in the down position indicating the gun was in action when it was hit. The Panther is finished in a monochrome coat of dark yellow, and the large red and white outlined turret numbers suggest it is from the Panzer-Lehr Division, which saw significant losses in the last year of the war.

(**Above**) A dead grenadier has been purposely laid over the 7.5cm barrel of a StuG.III assault gun while two US soldiers look on.

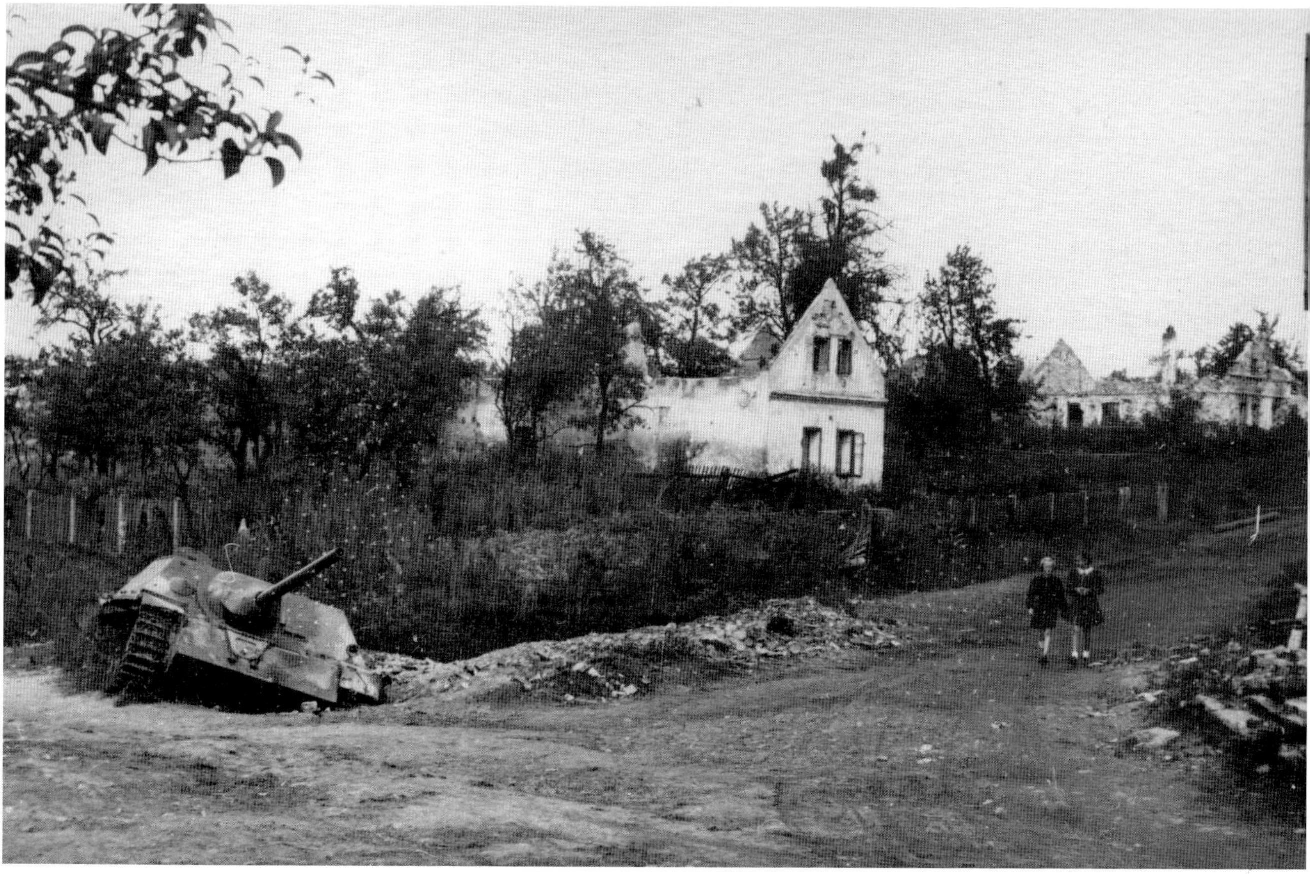

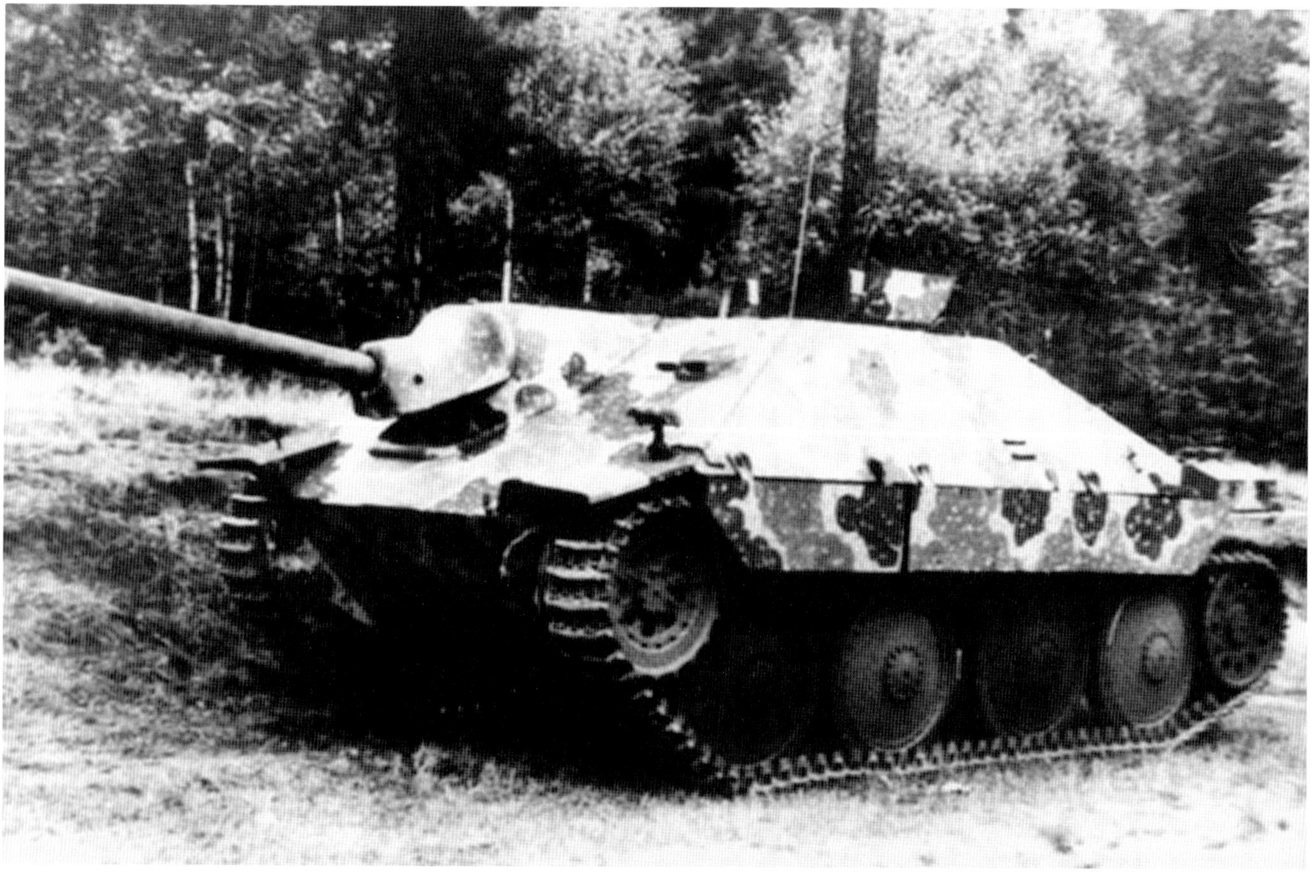

(**Opposite, above**) A Jagdpanzer IV, designated as 'Jagdpanzer IV A-0'. The vehicle sits derelict at the side of a junction in a ditch after evidently being knocked out of action. The tank destroyer mounts a powerful 7.5cm PaK 39 L/48.

(**Opposite, below**) An abandoned Hetzer in 1945. This vehicle undertook sterling service during the last months of the war. However, like all the German armour employed on the front lines, they were too few and dispersed to achieve little more than temporarily holding back the enemy.

(**Above**) There were a number of these Sturmpanzer IV 'Brummbar' vehicles employed on the Western Front between during the latter part of the war. This late production vehicle has been knocked out of action and been cannibalised for parts.

(**Above**) American troops sprawl out a German newspaper across the front plate of an abandoned StuG.III assault gun. Note the variety of German weapons captured leaning against the vehicle, comprising MG42 and MG34 machine guns.

(**Opposite, above**) In a decimated town a battery of Marder IIIs have been knocked out of action, more than likely by an aerial attack. In the last year of the war, with virtually no Luftwaffe support, German armour succumbed to huge losses. The situation became so bad by mid-1944 the Panzerwaffe were compelled to move their armour mainly at night to avoid being attacked.

(**Opposite, below**) A rare photograph of what appears to be an abandoned pre-production version of the Jagdpanzer IV, designated as the Jagdpanzer IV A–O. It has a curved superstructure front and is armed with two MG ports as well as a muzzle brake on the 7.5cm PaK 39 L/48 cannon.

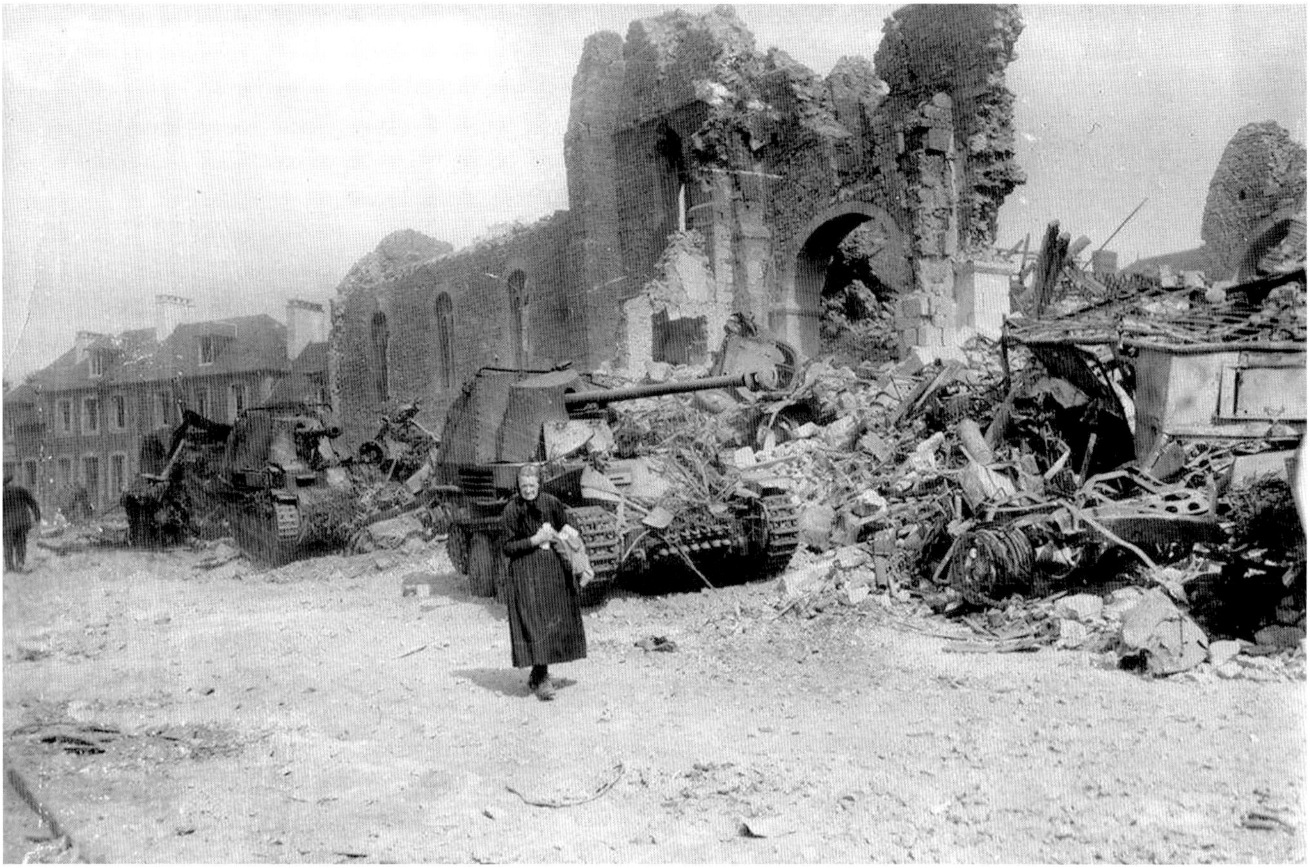

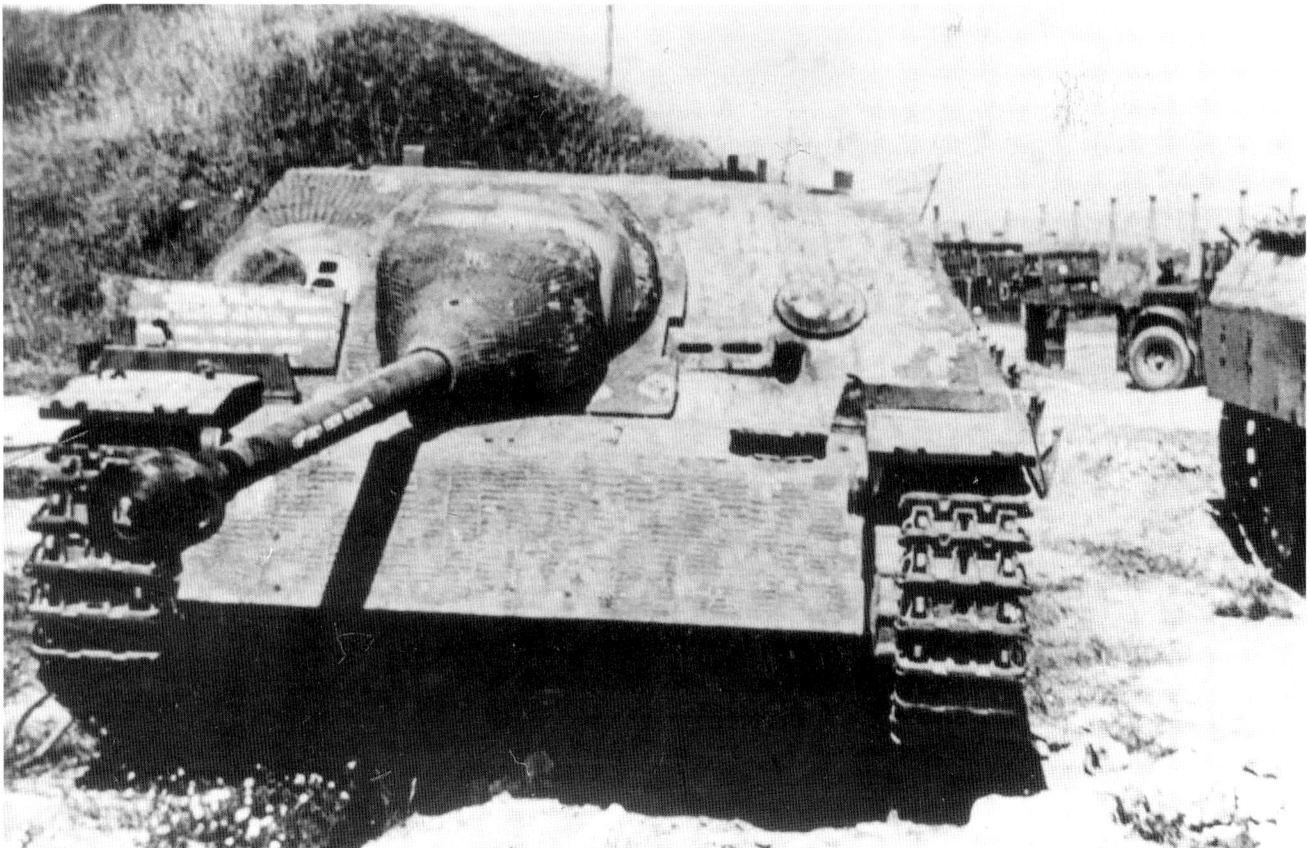

Hundreds of dejected German PoWs file through a gutted German town, flanked by their US captors.

Appendix One

Weapons Composition 1944

Artillery Regiment 1944
3 × 2cm FlaK Guns towed by a howitzer battalion
3 × 2cm FlaK Guns
4 × 15cm sFH 18 Howitzers
4 × 10.5cm leFH 18 Howitzers
1 battery of 6 × Hummels
2 batteries of 6 × Wespes
1 Company of 14 × Jagdpanzers
15 × 7.5cm PaK 40 vehicle-towed guns
1 Company of 12 × Quad FlaK 2cm guns
2 Companies of 4 × 8.8cm Guns

Armoured Reconnaissance Battalion 1944
4 platoons of 4 × Sd.Kfz.231
MG platoons of 4 × MG34/42 (on sustained fire mounts)
3 × rifle platoons

Armoured Reconnaissance Battalion Support 1944
2 × 7.5cm le IG 18 Guns
3 × 5cm PaK 38 Guns
1 × Engineer Platoon

Typical Panzer Division 1944 (15,943 men)
91 × Panzer IV (7.5cm L/48 guns) medium tanks
90 × Panther (7.5cm L/70 guns) medium tanks
42 × Hetzer (7.5cm L/48 guns) tank destroyers
9 × 15cm FH 18/40 towed howitzers
18 × 10.5cm leF 18 towed howitzers
6 × 15cm self-propelled sIG infantry guns
12 × 7.5cm PaK 40 towed anti-tank guns

36 × 5cm PaK 39 towed anti-tank guns
14 × 8.8cm FlaK 36 towed anti-aircraft guns
12 × 3.7cm FlaK 36 towed anti-aircraft guns
13 × 2cm towed anti-aircraft guns
32 × 7.5cm le.IG 37 and sIG 33 towed infantry guns
80 × 8.1cm mortars
570 × machine guns
48 × Sd.Kfz.232 and 263 armoured cars
1,000 × trucks

Appendix Two

Composition of an Infantry and Panzergrenadier Division

Infantry Division, 1944

By 1944 the infantry division had gone through a series of changes and had been modified and reorganised. The reconnaissance battalion for instance was removed and reintroduced with a bicycle mounted reconnaissance platoon within every regiment. The anti-tank battalion was more or less made motorised and consisted of an anti-tank company equipped with Jagdpanzer IVs, Hetzers or StuGs, which were organised into three platoons of four vehicles and an HQ section of two vehicles, a motorised anti-tank company of twelve 7.5cm PaK 40 guns and a motorised FlaK company equipped with twelve 2cm or 3.7cm FlaK guns. The engineer Battalion also took over the responsibility of the heavy weapons company. It comprised of three engineer companies, each equipped with two 81cm mortars, two MGs and six portable flamethrowers. The heavy weapons in the engineer battalion was normally mounted in trucks, but by 1944 they were predominately pulled by animal draught, while the troops would be mounted on bicycles.

At regimental level an anti-tank company was added. This consisted of a platoon equipped with three 5cm PaK 38 guns and two platoons armed with Panzerfausts. Within the regiments, the infantry battalions were reduced in size to just two. A number of divisions in the field were attached with fusilier battalions and were structured identically to the new standard rifle battalion. The infantry battalions were equipped with four 12cm heavy mortars, while the rifle companies' heavy weapons platoon were equipped with two 8.1cm mortars.

The Panzergrenadier Division, 1944

By 1944 many infantry divisions were redesignated as Panzergrenadier divisions. Although having an armoured designation, the Panzergrenadier division was still technically an infantry formation. However, unlike a normal infantry division there was a higher than usual attachment of armoured vehicles. A typical Panzergrenadier division had at least one battalion of infantry that were transported to the forward edge of the battlefield by Sd.Kfz.251 halftracks, and various armoured support provided by its own StuG Battalion. A typical Panzergrenadier division normally composed an HQ company, a motorised engineer battalion and two Panzergrenadier regiments. Invariably a Panzergrenadier division had a StuG Battalion, which contained an HQ Platoon equipped with three StuGs and three StuG Companies. The StuG battalion was normally supported by a company comprising of a StuG platoon which was equipped with four StuGs with 10.5cm guns, a FlaK platoon with three quad 2cm guns mounted on Sd.Kfz.6 or 7 halftracks, an armoured engineer platoon with five Sd.Kfz.250 halftracks, and a motorised signal platoon.

Panzer/Panzergrenadier-Brigade July 1944

By early July 1944 as the situation on the Western Front deteriorated, Hitler outlined that his forces needed small, mobile, fast armoured Kampfgruppe, which could be used effectively in action to meet the attacking enemy's armoured formations. During the first week of July plans were issued to create these special armoured Kampfgruppe. They were to consist of at least one SPW-Battalion; one Panzer group with some forty Panzers, one PaK Company and a number of FlaK wagons. In total about twelve such Kampfgruppe, named as Panzer-Brigades, were to be issued to fighting units on the Eastern Front.

On 11 July OKH issued orders to create ten Panzer-Brigades, to be designated Panzer-Brigade 101 to 110. Each Panzer-Brigade had one Panzer Abteilung with three Panther companies and one Panzer Jaeger company, one Panzergrenadier battalion with four companies.

Order of Battle: 6th June 1944

OB West (General Field Marshal von Rundstedt – Chief of Staff: General Blumentritt)

LXXXVIII Armeekorps (General Hans Wolfgang Reinhard – Chief of Staff: General Curt von Eichert-Wiersdorff)
347 Infanterie-Division (General Wolf Trierenberg)
16 Luftwaffen-Feld-Division (General Karl Sievers)
719 Infanterie-Division (General Karl Wahle)

Heeresgruppe B (General Field Marshal Rommel – Chief of Staff: General Hans Speidel)

15 Armee (General Hans von Salmuth)

LXXXIX Armeekorps (General Werner Freiherr von Gilsa)
70 Infanterie-Division (General Wilhelm Daser)
712 Infanterie-Division (General Friedrich Wilhelm Neumann)
48 Infanterie-Division (General Karl Casper)

LXXXII Armeekorps (General Johann Sinnhuber)
18 Luftwaffen-Feld-Division (General Joachim von Tresckow)
47 Infanterie-Division (General Otto Elfeldt)
49 Infanterie-Division (General Sigfrid Macholz)

LXVII Armeekorps (General Alfred Gause)
344 Infanterie-Division (General Eugen-Felix Schwalbe)
348 Infanterie-Division (General Paul Seyffardt)

LXXXI Armeekorps (General Adolf Kuntzen)
245 Infanterie-Division (General Erwin Sander)
17 Luftwaffen-Feld-Division (General Hans Kurt Hoecker)
711 Infanterie-Division (General Josef Reichert)

Army Reserves
19 Luftwaffen-Feld-Division (General Erich Baessler)
84 Infanterie-Division (General Erwin Menny)
85 Infanterie-Division (General Kurt Chill)
182 Reserve-Infanterie-Division (General Richard Baltzer)
326 Infanterie-Division (General Viktor von Drabich-Waechter)
331 Infanterie-Division (General Heinz Furbach)
346 Infanterie-Division (General Erich Diestel)

7 Armee (General Friedrich Dollmann)

LXXXIV Armeekorps (General Erich Marcks)
716 Infanterie-Division (General Wilhelm Richter)
352 Infanterie-Division (General Dietrich Kraiss)
709 Infanterie-Division (General Karl-Wilhelm von Schlieben)
319 Infanterie-Division (General Rudolf graf von Schmettow)
Ostregimentstab 752 (Oberst Julius Coretti)

74th Armeekorps (General Erich Straube)
77 Infanterie-Division (General Rudolf Stegmann)
266 Infanterie-Division (General Karl Spang)

XXV Armeekorps (General Wilhelm Fahrmbacher)
343 Infanterie-Division (General Erwin Rauch)
265 Infanterie-Division (General Walther Duevert)
275 Infanterie-Division (General Hans Schmidt)

Army Reserve
30 Schnelle-Brigade (Oberstleutnant freiherr von Aufsess)
91 Luftlande-Division (General Wilhelm Falley)
243 Infanterie-Division (General Heinz Hellmich)
II Fallschirmjäger-Korps (General Fallschirmjäger Eugen Meindl)
3 Fallschirmjäger-Division (General Richard Schimpf)
5 Fallschirmjäger-Division (General Gustav Wilke)

Armeegruppe G (General Johannes Blaskowitz)
1 Armee (General Joachim Lemelsen)

LXXX Armeekorps (General Kurt Gallenkamp)
158 Reserve-Infanterie-Division (General Ernst Haeckel)
708 Infanterie-Division (General Hermann Wilck)

LXXXVI Armeekorps (General Hans von Obstfelder)
159 Reserve-Infanterie-Division (General Hermann Meyer-Rabingen)
276 Infanterie-Division (General Curt Badinski)

19th Armee (General Georg von Sodenstern)

IV Luftwaffe-Feldkorps (General Erich Petersen)
272 Infanterie-Division (General Friedrich August Schack)
277 Infanterie-Division (General Albert Praun)
271 Infanterie-Division (General Paul Danhauser)

44 LXXXV Armeekorps (General Baptist Kniess)
338 Infanterie-Division (General René de l'Homme de Courbière)
244 Infanterie-Division (General Hans Schaefer)

LXII Reserve-Armeekorps (General Ferdinand Neuling)
242 Infanterie-Division (General Johannes Baessler)
157 Reserve-Infanterie-Division (General Karl Pflaum)

Panzergruppe West (General Leo Geyr freiherr von Schweppenburg)

I SS-Panzerkorps (Obergruppenfuhrer Josef 'Sepp' Dietrich)
1 SS-Panzer-Division
17 SS-Panzergrenadier-Division (SS-Oberführer Werner Ostendorff)
Panzer-Lehr-Division (General Fritz Bayerlein)

LVIII Reserve-Panzerkorps (General Walter Krueger)
189 Reserve-Infanterie-Division (General Richard von Schwerin)
2 SS-Panzer-Division (SS Brigadeführer Heinz Lammerding)
9 Panzer-Division (General Erwin Jolasse)
LXVI Reserve-Armeekorps (General Hans freiherr von Funck)
2 Panzer-Division (General Heinrich freiherr von Luettwitz)
21 Panzer-Division (General Edgar Feuchtinger)
116 Panzer-Division (General Gerhard Graf von Schwerin)
11 Panzer-Division (General Wend von Wietersheim)

Appendix Four

Order of Battle: Holland, September 1944

Army Group B (General Field Marshal Walther Model)

II SS Panzer Korps (SS-Obergruppenführer Wilhelm Bittrich)
9 SS Panzer-Division Hohenstaufen (SS-Obersturmbannführer Walter Harzer)
9 SS Panzer-Regiment
19 SS-Panzergrenadier-Regiment
20 SS-Panzergrenadier-Regiment
9 SS Artillery Regiment
9th SS Aufk Battalion
9 SS PaK Battalion
9 SS Engineer Battalion
9 SS FlaK Battalion
9 SS Signals Battalion
10 SS Panzer-Division 'Frundsberg' (SS-Brigadeführer Heinz Harmel)
10 SS-Panzer-Regiment
21 SS Panzergrenadier-Regiment
22 SS Panzergrenadier-Regiment
10 SS Artillery Regiment
10 SS Recon Battalion
10 SS PaK Battalion
10 SS Engineer Battalion
10 SS FlaK Battalion
10 SS Signals Battalion
Training regiment of Fallschirm-Panzer Division 1 Hermann Göring (Oberstleutnant Fritz Fullriede)
Kampfgruppe 'Von Tettau' (Generalleutnant Hans von Tettau)
Kampfgruppe 'Kraft' (SS-Sturmbannführer Sepp Kraft of Training and Replacement Battalion 16)
Kampfgruppe 'Henke'

15th Armee (General Gustav-Adolf von Zangen)

LXVIII Korps (General Otto Sponheimer)
346 Infantry-Division (General Erich Diestel)
711 Static-Division (General Josef Reichert)
719 Coastal Division (General Karl Sievers)

LXXXVIII Korps (General Hans-Wolfgang Reinhard)
Kampfgruppe 'Chill' (General Kurt Chill)
59 Infantry-Division (General Walter Poppe)
245 Infantry-Division (Oberst Gerhard Kegler)
712 Static-Division (General Friedrich-Wilhelm Neumann)

LXXXVI Korps (General Hans von Obstfelder)
176 Infanterie (Oberst Christian Landau)
Kampfgruppe 'Walther'
6 Fallschirmjäger-Regiment (Oberst Friedrich August Freiherr von der Heydte)
107 Panzer-Brigade (Major Freiherr von Maltzahn)
Division 'Erdmann' (General Wolfgang Erdmann)

XII SS Korps (SS-Obergruppenführer: Curt von Gottberg)
180 Infantry-Division (General Bernhard Klosterkemper)
190 Infantry-Division (General Ernst Hammer)
363 Volksgrenadier-Division (General Augustus Dettling)

Wehrkreis VI
Corps 'Feldt' (General Kurt Feldt)
406 Landesschützen-Division (General Scherbenning)

Luftwaffe West (Colonel General Kurt Student)
1 Fallschirmtruppen Armee
I Fallschirmtruppen Korps
II Fallschirmtruppen Korps (General Eugen Meindl)
86 Korps

Order of Battle: Ardennes, 15 December 1944

Heeresgruppe B (General Field Marshal Walter Model)

Units

III FlaK Korps (General Wolfgang Pickert)
813 Panzer Pionier Kompanie
725 Eisenbahn Artillerie-Abteilung
674 Eisenbahn Artillerie-Abteilung
688 Eisenbahn Artillerie-Abteilung
749 Eisenbahn Artillerie-Abteilung

OKW Reserve

79 Volksgrenadier-Division (General Alois Weber)
257 Volksgrenadier-Division (General Erich Seidel)
11 Panzer-Division (General Wend von Wietersheim)
3 Panzergrenadier-Division (General Walter Denkert)
6 SS-Gebirgs-Division (SS-Gruppenführer Karl-Heinrich Brenner)
10 SS-Panzer-Division (SS-Brigadeführer Heinz Harmel)

5th Panzer-Armee (General der Panzertruppen Hasso-Eccard von Manteuffel)

Units

9 FlaK-Brigade (Oberst Paul Schluchtmann)
1 FlaK-Sturm-Regiment
182 FlaK-Regiment Volks-Artillerie-Korps
410 Führer-Begleit-Brigade (Oberst Bremer)

XXXXVII Panzer-Korps (General Freiherr Heinrich von Lüttwitz)
Panzer-Lehr-Division (General Fritz Bayerlein)
901 Panzergrenadier-Regiment (Oberst Scholze)
902 Panzergrenadier-Regiment (Oberst Gutmann
130 Panzer-Regiment

130 Panzer-Artillery-Regiment (Oberst Luxenberger)
130 Panzer-Aufklärungs-Abteilung (Major von Born-Fallois)
311 Panzer-FlaK-Artillerie-Abteilung
130 Panzer-Jäger-Abteilung
130 Panzer-Pioneer-Battalion (Major Brandt)
130 Panzer-Nachrichten-Abteilung
26 Volksgrenadier-Division (Generalmajor Heinz Kokott)
9 Panzer-Division (General Freiherr von Harald Elverfeldt)
15 Panzergrenadier-Division (General Hans-Joachim Deckert)
182 FlaK-Regiment

XXXIX Panzer-Korps (General Karl Decker)
167 Volksgrenadier-Division (General Hanskurt Hocker)
1 SS-Panzer-Division (SS-Brigadeführer Wilhelm Mohnke)
10 SS-Panzer-Division (SS-Brigadeführer Heinz Harmel)
7 Fallschirmjäger Division (General Wolfgang Erdmann)
StuG Brigade 394
StuG Artillerie Brigade 667

LVIII Armee-Korps (General Walter Krueger)
560 Volksgrenadier-Division (Generalmajor Rudolf Bader)
116 Panzer-Division (General Siegfried von Waldenburg)

2 Panzer-Division (General Meinrad von Lauchert)

LXVI Armee-Korps (General Walther Lucht)
18 Volksgrenadier-Division (General Gunther Hoffmann-Schonborn)
62 Volksgrenadier-Division (General Fritz Warnecke Führer-Begleit-Brigade)

6 Panzer-Armee (SS-Oberst-Gruppenführer Josef Dietrich)

Units
Skorzeny Brigade 150 (SS-Obersturmbannführer Otto Skorzeny)
Volks-Artillerie-Korps
Volks-Werfer-Brigade
2 FlaK Division (Oberst Fritz Laicher)
246 Volksgrenadier-Division

LXVII Armee Korps (General Otto Hitzfeld)
272 Volksgrenadier-Division (General Eugen Konig)
326 Volksgrenadier-Division (General Dr Erwin Kaschner)
2 FlaK-Sturm-Regiment

LXVI Armee Korps (General Walther Lucht)
12 Volksgrenadier-Division (General Gerhard Engel)
62 Volksgrenadier-Division (General Fritz Warnecke)
560 Volksgrenadier-Division (General Rudolf Bader)

Korps Felber (General Hans Felber)
18 Volksgrenadier-Division (General Gunther)
62 Volksgrenadier-Division (General Fritz Warnecke)

I SS-Panzer Korps (SS Gruppenführer Hermann Priess)

Units
277 Volksgrenadier-Division (General Wilhelm Viebig)
I SS-Pz.Gre.Rgt.25 (SS-Hauptsturmführer Ott)
12 Volksgrenadier-Division (General Gerhard Engel)
Grenadier-Regiment 48 (Oberst Wilhelm Osterhold)
Grenadier-Regiment 89 (Oberst Gerhard Lemcke)
Fusilier Regiment 27 (Oberst Heinz-Georg Lemm)
3 FlaK-Sturm-Regiment
4 FlaK-Sturm-Regiment
340 Volksgrenadier-Division (General Theodor Tolsdorff)
3 Fallschirmjäger Division (General Walter Wadehn)

1 SS-Panzer Division (SS-Brigadeführer Wilhelm Mohnke)

16 December 1944
Stabskompanie (SS-Obersturmführer Goltz)
2 Kompanie (SS-Obersturmführer Coblenz)
3 Kompanie (SS-Obersturmführer Leidreiter)
4 Kompanie (SS-Obersturmführer Wagner)
Versuchs-Komp (SS-Obersturmführer Reuss)
2 SS-Panzer-Pionier-Abteilung 1 (SS-Untersturmführer Unglaube)
2 SS-Panzer-Artillerie-Regiment 1 (SS-Obersturmführer Butschek)
12 SS-Panzer Division (SS-Brigadeführer Hugo Kraas)
Schwere Panzerjager Abteilung 559
Schwere Panzerjager Abteilung 560 (Major Streger)
Divisions-begleit-kompanie (SS-Untersturmführer Stier)
SS-Pz.Rgt.12 (SS-Sturmbannführer Kuhlmann – Adjutant: SS-Obersturmführer
    von Ribbentrop)
I Abteilung (SS-Sturmbannführer Jurgensen died 23.12.44, then
    SS-Obersturmführer von Ribbentrop)
1–4 Kompanie

II Abteilung (SS-Hauptsturmführer Seigel)

5–9 Kompanie

SS-Panzergrenadier-Regiment 25 (SS-Sturmbannführer S. Muller)

SS-Panzer-Aufklärungs-Abteilung 2 'Das Reich' (SS-Sturmbannführer Ernst Krag)

9(arm) SS-Panzer-Grenadier-Regiment 4 'Der Führer'

III SS-Panzer-Artillerie-Regiment 2 'Das Reich' (SS-Hauptsturmführer Herbert
    Hoffmann)

Divisions-Sturmkompanie

I Bataillon (SS-Hauptsturmführer Ott – Adjutant: SS-Obersturmführer Klein)

1–4 Kompanie

II Bataillon (SS-Obersturmbannführer Schulze then SS-Hauptsturmführer Damsch)

5–8 Kompanie

III Bataillon (SS-Hauptsturmführer Bruckner – Adjutant: SS-Untersturmführer Schauble)

9–12 Kompanie

SS-Panzergrenadier-Regiment Regiment 26 (SS-Sturmbannführer Krause –
    Adjutant: SS-Obersturmführer Holzl)

1–4 Kompanie

II Bataillon (SS-Hauptsturmführer Hauschild – Adjutant: SS-Obersturmführer Lubbe)

5–8 Kompanie

III Bataillon (SS-Hauptsturmführer Urabl, Adjutant: SS-Obersturmführer Kugler)

9–12 Kompanie

SS-Werfer Abteilung 12 (SS-W.Muller, Adjutant: SS-Obersturmführer Lämmerhirt)

1–4 Batterie

SS-FlaK Abteilung 12 (SS-Sturmbannführer Dr Loenicker – Adjutant:
    SS-Untersturmführer Kolb)

1–5 Batterie

SS-Aufklärungs Abteilung 12 (SS-Sturmbannführer Bremer)

1–5 Kompanie

SS-Artillerie Regiment 12 (SS-Obersturmbannführer Drexler – Adjutant:
    SS-Hauptsturmführer Macke)

SS-Panzer-Jäger-Abteilung 12 (SS-Hauptsturmführer Brockschmidt – Adjutant:
    SS-Untersturmführer Protst)

1–3 Kompanie

Kampfgruppe Zeine

1 Panzer-Jäger-Abteilung 12 (SS-Obersturmführer Zeine)

Kampfgruppe Kuhlmann

Staff of Panzer-Regiment 12

I Panzer-Grenadier-Regiment 26 (SS-Sturmbannführer Hein)

II Artillerie-Regiment 12 (SS-Sturmbannführer Neumann)
Schwere Panzer-Jäger-Abteilung 560 (Major Streger)

II SS-Panzer Korps (SS-Obergruppenführer Wilhelm Bittrich)
2 SS-Panzer-Division (SS-Brigadeführer Heinz Lammerding)
9 SS-Panzer-Division
10 SS-Panzer-Division
Schwere SS-Panzerabteilung 102/502 (SS-Sturmbannführer Kurt Hartrampf)
SS-Werfer-Abteilung 102/502 (SS-Hauptsturmführer Alfred Nickmann)
560 Volksgrenadier-Division
116 Panzer Division
12 SS Panzer-Division 'Hitlerjugend'
3 Fallschirmjäger-Division
277 Volksgrenadier-Division
3 Panzergrenadier-Division

7 Armee (General der Panzertruppen Erich Brandenberger)

Units
FlaK-Regiment 15

LIII Armee Korps (General Kavallerie Edwin Graf von Rothkirch und Trach)
Security Battalions
Engineer Brigade 47
26 Volksgrenadier-Division (General Heinz Kokott)
9 Volksgrenadier-Division (General Werner Kolb)
79 Volksgrenadier-Division (General Alois Weber)
167 Volksgrenadier-Division (General Hanskurt Hocker)
276 Volksgrenadier-Division (General Hugo Dempwolf)
5 Fallschirmjäger Division (General Sebastian Ludwig Heilmann)
1 FlaK Brigade
Fuhrer-Grenadier-Brigade

LXXXV Armee Korps (General Smilo Freiherr von Lüttwitz)
352 Volksgrenadier-Division (General Richard Bazing)
5 Fallschirmjäger Division (General Sebastian Ludwig Heilmann)

15 Armee (General Gustav-Adolf von Zangen)

Units
1 FlaK Brigade (Oberst Oskar Schottl)
Schwere Panzerabteilung 506 (Major Lange)
FlaK Regiment 18

XII SS-Armee Korps (General Gunther Blumentritt)
183 Volksgrenadier-Division (General Wolfgang Lange)
176 Volksgrenadier-Division (General Christian-Johannes-Landau)
59 Volksgrenadier-Division (General Walter Poppe)
Volks-Artillerie-Korps 407 (Oberst Hermann Seidel)

Korps Felber
340 Volksgrenadier-Division (General Theodor Tolsdorff)

LXXXI Armee Korps (General der Friedrich Kochling)
363 Volksgrenadier-Division (General August Dettling)
246 Volksgrenadier-Division (General Peter Korte)
47 Volksgrenadier-Division (General Max Bork)

Korps attachments
Volks-Artillerie-Korps 409 (Oberst Willibald Neudecker)
Schwere Panzer-Abteilung 301 (Hauptmann Kramer)
Panzer-Abteilung 319
StuG Brigade 341
Schwere Panzer-Abteilung 682

LXXIV Armee Korps (General Karl Puchler)
353 Infantry-Division (General Paul Mahlmann)
85 Infantry-Division (General Helmut Bechler)
89 Infantry-Division (General Walter Burns)

Korps attachments
StuG Brigade 394 (Hauptmann Gerd Schmock)
344 Infantry-Division
Kampfgruppe Peiper
SS-Panzer Regiment 1 'LSSAH' (SS-Obersturmbannführer Jochen Peiper)
I SS-Panzer-Regiment 1 (SS-Sturmbannführer Werner Pötschke)
HQ Company I SS-Panzer-Regiment 1 (SS-Rolf Buchheim)
Supply Company I SS-Panzer-Regiment 1 (SS-Ernst Otto)
1 SS-Panzer-Regiment 1 (SS-Obersturmführer Karl Kremser)
2 SS-Panzer-Regiment 1 (SS-Obersturmführer Friedrich Christ)
6 SS-Panzer-Regiment 1 (SS-Obersturmführer Benoni Junker)
Schwere SS-Panzer-Abteilung 501 (SS-Obersturmbannführer Heinz von
    Westernhagen, Tiger 007 – Adjutant: SS-Untersturmführer Eduard Kalinowsky
    Tiger 008)
Supply Company SS-Panzer-Abteilung 501 (SS-Obersturmführer Paul Vogt)
1 SS-Panzer-Abteilung 501 (SS-Obersturmführer Jurgen Wessel, Tiger 105)

2 SS-Panzer-Abteilung 501 (SS-Hauptsturmführer Rolf Mobius, Tiger 205)

3 SS-Panzer-Abteilung 501 (SS-Hauptsturmführer Heinz Birnschein)

7 SS-Panzer-Regiment 1 (SS-Hauptsturmführer Oskar Klingelhofer)

9 SS-Panzer-Regiment 1 (SS-Obersturmführer Erich Rumpf)

10 (FlaK) SS-Panzer-Regiment 1 (SS-Obersturmführer Karl-Heinz Vogler)

Maintenance company, SS-Panzer-Regiment 1 (SS-Obersturmführer Wilhelm Ratschko)

III Gepanzerte SS-Panzer-Grenadier-Regiment 2 (SS-Hauptsturmführer Josef Diefenthal)

9 Gepanzerte SS-Panzer-Grenadier-Regiment 2 (SS-Untersturmführer Max Leike)

10 Gepanzerte SS-Panzer-Grenadier-Regiment 2 (SS-Obersturmführer Georg Preuss)

11 Gepanzerte SS-Panzer-Grenadier-Regiment 2 (SS-Obersturmführer Heinz Tomhardt)

12 Gepanzerte SS-Panzer-Grenadier-Regiment 2 (SS-Hauptscharführer Jochen Thiele)

4 (leichte) SS Panzer-Abteilung 501 (SS-Hauptsturmführer Wilhelm Spitz)

Supply company, III SS-Panzer-Grenadier-Regiment 2 (SS-Obersturmführer Wolfgang Lüdecke)

13 (IG) SS-Panzer-Grenadier-Regiment 2 (SS-Obersturmführer Koch)

3 Gepanzerte SS-Panzer-Pionier-Bataillon 1 (SS-Obersturmführer Franz Sievers)

FlaK Abteilung 84 (Major von Sacken)

1–4 Batterie

Fallschirmjäger Regiment 9 (Oberst von Hoffmann)

I Regiment 9 (Hauptmann Fritz Schiffke)

II Regiment 9 (Major Taubert)

Kampfgruppe Krag

SS-Panzer-Aufklarungs-Abteilung 2 (SS-Sturmbannführer Ernst Krag)

2 SS-Sturmgeschütz-Abteilung

1 SS-Panzer-Pionier-Battalion 2

I SS-Panzer-Artillerie-Regiment 2 (SS-Hauptsturmführer Herbert Hoffmann)

One Medical Support Zug

Appendix Six

Order of Battle: Defence on the Western Front, March & April 1945

Wehr.Befh. Denmark

Stab ZBV
Division North Jutland
160 Infanterie-Division
233 Panzer-Division
OB Northwest
Fuhrungs-Stab North Coast

OB Netherlands
OB Reserves:
Stab 331 Infanterie-Division
XXX (30) Armeekorps:
249 Infanterie-Division
Stab 20 ZBV Brigade

34 SS-Division 'Landsturm-Niederlande'

88 Armeekorps:
346 Infanterie-Division (most)
361 Infanterie-Division

6 Fallschirmjäger-Division
149 Infanterie-Division

FIRST PARACHUTE ARMY

II (02) Fallschirmjäger Korps:
8 Fallschirmjäger-Division
7 Fallschirmjäger-Division and
    346 Infanterie-Division
245 Infanterie-Division

86 Armeekorps
GD Panzer-Verband
Division 471 and Division 490
325 Schatten-Division
15 Panzergrenadier-Division

ARMEEGRUPPE Blumentritt

Korps Stab Ems
Division 480
172 ZBV Division

2 Marine Infanterie-Division
Stellvertreter 11 Armeekorps
3 Panzergrenadier-Division (Kampfgruppe)

HEERESGRUPPE B

Heeresgruppe Reserves:
326 Volksgrenadier-Division
340 Volksgrenadier-Division

5 Fallschirmjäger-Division
166 Infanterie-Division

ARMEE ABTEILUNG Von Lüttwitz

47 Panzerkorps
53 Armeekorps:
116 Panzer-Division (most)
22 FlaK-Division
190 Infanterie-Division

180 Infanterie-Division
Group Von Deichmann
63 Armeekorps
2 Fallschirmjäger-Division
Stab Infanterie-Division Hamburg

FIFTH PANZER ARMY

12 SS-Korps
363 Infanterie-Division
Stab Group Witte
3 Fallschirmjäger-Division (Kampfgruppe)
59 Infanterie-Division
58 Panzerkorps

183 Volksgrenadier-Division
9 Panzer-Division
12 Volksgrenadier-Division
353 Infanterie-Division
62 Volksgrenadier-Division

FIFTEENTH ARMY

74 Armeekorps:
272 Volksgrenadier-Division
3 Panzergrenadier-Division
Group Meissner

Panzer-Division Lehr
176 Infanterie-Division
338 Infanterie-Division

OB – WEST

OB Reserves:
63 Infanterie-Division
89 Infanterie-Division
150 Infanterie-Division
151 Infanterie-Division
18 Volksgrenadier-Division
167 Infanterie-Division
Division 476

Stab AOK 11
Stab AOK 24
Group Weissenberger
Stab Division 407
WKrs VII
WKrs VI
Division 406
Division 476

ELEVENTH ARMY

66 Armeekorps
116 Panzer-Division (Kampfgruppe)
9 Panzer-Division (Kampfgruppe)
SS-Panzer-Brigade Westfalen
277 Volksgrenadier-Division
Stellvertreter 9 Armeekorps
326 Volksgrenadier-Division

26 Volksgrenadier-Division
67 Armeekorps:
Group Grosskreuz
Group Heidenreich
Group Ettner
Group Feller

HEERESGRUPPE G

Heeresgruppe Reserves
Stab 89 Armeekorps
352 Volksgrenadier-Division
905 zur besonderen Verwendung-
   Division

347 Volksgrenadier-Division
159 Infanterie-Division
276 Volksgrenadier-Division

SEVENTH ARMY

AOK Reserves
6 SS-Gebirgs-Division Nord
90 Armeekorps
Local Alarm Units
85 Armeekorps
11 Panzer Division
Group Schroeter
12 Armeekorps

Group Von Berg
2 Panzer Division
82 Armeekorps
36 Volksgrenadier-Division and
   256 Volksgrenadier-Division
21 FlaK-Division
Division 416

FIRST ARMY

13 SS-Korps
Panzer Brigade Von Hube
Division Bayern
79 Volksgrenadier-Division
212 Volksgrenadier-Division
Stab 9 Volksgrenadier-Division
Infanterie-Division Alpen
Stab 616 zur besonderen
   Verwendung-Division

13 Armeekorps
553 Volksgrenadier-Division
17 SS-Panzer-Grenadier-Division
   (Götz von Berlichingen)
246 Volksgrenadier-Division
19 Volksgrenadier-Division
2 Gebirg-Division

NINETEENTH ARMY

AOK Reserves
189 Infanterie-Division
18 SS-Korps
Division 405

Division 805
1005 Infanterie-Brigade
Infanterie-Brigade (Bauer)

80 Armeekorps

559 Volksgrenadier-Division
198 Infanterie-Division

47 Volksgrenadier-Division
16 Volksgrenadier-Division

64 Armeekorps

716 Infanterie-Division
257 Volksgrenadier-Division

106 Infanterie-Division

Marine Obkdo West

Ob Reserves
319 Infanterie-Division
226 Infanterie-Division (Kampfgruppe)

25 Armeekorps Lorient
265 Infanterie-Division

OKW – RESERVES

Rear Heeresgruppe B
41 Panzerkorps
39 Panzerkorps
20 Armeekorps
OKW Reserves Forming
Infanterie-Division Potsdam 85
Infanterie-Division (Ulrich von Hutten)
1 Reichsarbeitsdienst-Division
   (Schlageter)
2 Reichsarbeitsdienst-Division (Friedrich
   Ludwig Jahn)
3 Reichsarbeitsdienst-Division (Theodor
   Korner)

Panzer Division Clausewitz
O.B.d.E.
599 Infanterie-Brigade
599 Infanterie-Division
48 Infanterie-Division
264 Infanterie-Division
199 Infanterie-Division
SS-Führungshauptamt:
33 SS-Division Charlemagne
25 SS-Division Hungarian 1
26 SS-Division Hungarian 2
30 SS-Division Russian 1
38 SS-Division Nibelungen

Notes

Notes

Notes

Notes